JUNIOR CERTIFICATE

Romeo and Juliet

EDITED BY
Tom Brady

Gill & Macmillan

Gill & Macmillan Ltd
Hume Avenue, Park West
Dublin 12
with associated companies throughout the world
www.gillmacmillan.ie

ISBN-13: 978 07171 2822 8

Design and print origination in Ireland by O'K Graphic Design, Dublin
Colour reproduction by Typeform Repro Ltd, Dublin

*The paper used in this book is made from the wood pulp of managed forests. For every
tree felled, at least one tree is planted, thereby renewing natural resources.*

A catalogue record is available for this book from the British Library.

Contents

Acknowledgments

PHOTOGRAPHS
The photographs of the play in this book and on the front cover are by Donald Cooper, PhotoStage and are the photographer's copyright.
  They are from the 1995 production of *Romeo & Juliet* by the Royal Shakespeare Company.

DIRECTED BY Adrian Noble
DESIGNED BY Kendra Ullyart

Cast:

THE HOUSE OF MONTAGUE

Montague	Jeffrey Dench
Lady Montague	Anita Wright
Romeo	Zubin Varla
Benvolio	Michael Gould
Balthasar	Godfrey Walters

THE HOUSE OF CAPULET

Capulet	Christopher Benjamin
Lady Capulet	Darlene Johnson
Juliet	Lucy Whybrow
Tybalt	Dermot Kerrigan
Nurse	Susan Brown
Peter	Gary Taylor
Cousin Capulet	Christopher Robbie
Sampson	Justin Shevlin
Gregory	Paul Hilton

Chorus	Christopher Robbie
Escalus, Prince of Verona	Christopher Robbie
Mercutio	Mark Lockyer
Paris	Paul Bettany
Paris's Page	Ralph Birtwell
Friar Lawrence	Julian Glover
Apothecary	Jeffrey Dench
Rosaline	Lise Stevenson
Lady	Joanna Hole
Lady	Rachel Sanders
Captain of the Watch	Christopher Tune
Waiter	Ralph Birtwell
Children:	Holly Austen, Alexander Bennison, Francesca Bradley, Benjamin Hunt, Ferdinand Kingsley, Emilie-Jane Leconcq, Sam Whybrow

The photographs of the reconstructed Globe Theatre in the introduction, are from the International Globe Centre Ltd., New Globe Walk, Bankside, Southwark, London SE1 9DT.

PORTRAIT OF SHAKESPEARE: National Portrait Gallery, London

Introduction

WILLIAM SHAKESPEARE 1564–1616

William Shakespeare was the son of John Shakespeare, a respected and reasonably wealthy man who, in 1557, had married Mary Arden, the daughter of a distinguished Catholic family. William, their third child, was baptised in the Holy Trinity Church at Stratford-upon-Avon in 1564.

William received a good grammar school education. When he was eighteen, he married Ann Hathaway. She was a few years older than him. Five months after their wedding their first child, Suzanna, was born, followed two years later by the birth of twins, Hamnet and Judith, in 1585.

The reconstructed Globe Theatre in London

It is not known when Shakespeare first moved to London. However, it is clear that he went there to make a career for himself as an actor and then as a playwright. The first mention of him is by Robert Greene who describes Shakespeare as being 'an upstart . . . with his tiger's heart hid in a player's hide' who thinks he can write as well as any of his contemporaries. It was a criticism that revealed a jealousy born of the fear of a new writer who was beginning to make a name for himself.

During the 1590s, theatre — long regarded as entertainment suitable only for the lower classes — increased in popularity in London and began attracting the nobility. By 1594 there were three theatres in the city and Shakespeare's group of actors, known as the Lord Chamberlain's Company, was formed. (In 1603 it was renamed as the King's Players.) This company played at The Theatre, built for

James Burbage in 1576, which was the first theatre in London. In 1598, following a disagreement with the landlord, the company moved across the river to the newly built Globe Theatre, of which Shakespeare was a founder and director.

Shakespeare prospered throughout the 1590s and in 1597 he bought a large estate at Stratford called New Place. He retired there in 1610 and died in April 1616, having written thirty-seven plays and numerous poems.

William Shakespeare

BACKGROUND TO THE PLAY

The story of Romeo and Juliet originated in folklore and became well known to the English public through the Italian novelle (short prose tales) which were very popular in England in the late 1500s.

The tragic lovers' story appeared in a clearly defined form in a novella by Masuccio Salernitano in 1476. Salernitano claimed that it had a basis in truth. Many more Italian versions were written in the sixteenth century.

In 1562 Boaisteau's French version of the tale was translated into English for the first time by Arthur Brooke. Brooke's translation, with an emphasis on Fate and Fortune, was influenced by Chaucer's epic poem 'Troilus and Cressida'.

Shakespeare, who probably wrote his play *Romeo and Juliet* in 1595, was familiar with the various versions. He was particularly influenced by Brooke's adaptation, making great use of Brooke's accounts of the Italian setting and of Italian culture.

It is important to be aware that, although Shakespeare is writing his version of a well known tale, his *Romeo and Juliet* is very much an original play in its use of language, its focus on certain themes, and in its unique emphasis on relationships and exploration of the human condition.

Shakespeare fleshes out the parts of minor characters such as Benvolio, the Nurse, Mercutio and Tybalt. He develops the character of Paris to parallel Romeo as a rival suitor and reduces the action of the plot from months to five or six days.

In Shakespeare's hands, the play is rich in contrasts and complexities that were sometimes lost in the earlier versions, and which allow it a universal and timeless appeal.

A performance inside the reconstructed Globe Theatre

THE PLAY AS TRAGEDY

Romeo and Juliet is unusual among Shakespeare's tragedies in that it has two central protagonists — a hero and a heroine. Usually, Shakespearean tragedy, like the classical Greek tragedy of Sophocles and Euripedes, focuses on the plight of one heroic individual whose downfall is a result of his own actions.

This is not the case in *Romeo and Juliet*. Instead, this tragedy is about two youths whose lives seem to be controlled by Fate and the agents of Destiny and whose deaths are caused by the turmoil of the society in which they live. In other words, their misfortune is not brought about by defects of character, but by forces outside their control.

In having two central figures, Shakespeare risked dividing the sympathy of the audience and diminishing the intensity of the tragic experience. However, the counter argument is that the misfortunes of the hero and heroine mirror and counterpoint each other, so that theirs is so much a singular plight that we tend to view them almost as two sides of the same coin. In other words, the audience's sympathy is never divided between these two characters because we tend to respond to them as one.

DRAMA AND FICTION

SOME SIMILARITIES

There are many similarities between fiction and drama. Both of these writing forms usually deal with imagined worlds — places that have been invented by the author and peopled with imaginary characters. Furthermore, the lives of these characters follow a pattern that has been carefully decided by the author, so that they are lives that are realised rather than lived. However, while we are reading a novel or short story, or watching a play, we tend to *suspend disbelief* and enter into a fictional world willing to accept it as real. A large part of the enjoyment of these works derives from the fact that we become temporarily involved in the lives of the characters, interested in their destinies, the choices they make and their relationships. In this way, the manner in which we relate to the stories presented by fiction and drama are alike.

DIFFERENCES

The worlds of drama and fiction are, however, also dissimilar. The way in which a story is told is an essential difference that directly affects our responses to the work and how we engage with it.

The Differences in Telling the Story

Fiction, for example, is narrated either by the author or by some character in the story. How we understand and view the story is very much determined by the narrator and whether that teller of the tale is reliable (someone in whom the reader can trust and who acts as a moral guide) or unreliable (someone who is biased in presenting the reader with the tale and who cannot be trusted). So it can be said that our reading of fiction is influenced by the voice of the narrator.

Yet, with drama it is not usual to have a narrator in the strict sense of the word. Although there may be a chorus that introduces the action, provides a commentary or sets the scene, it is unusual to have a character who provides a constant commentary on the action, gives the reader descriptions of people, surroundings and objects, or sets the mood with descriptive passages. Part of the reason for this is that drama is essentially concerned with dialogue and with characters expressing themselves through the use of dialogue and changes of tone. The descriptive passages are unnecessary because the staging and the sets provide the audience with a visual impression that contributes to establishing mood.

The Difference in Experience

In fact, in considering that distinction, another important difference between fiction and drama is revealed. The reading of fiction tends to be a solitary activity, with the reader entering the world of the book almost privately. It is an intimate relationship in which the book casts its spell and the reader uses his or her imagination to conjure up the world described. However, drama is written to be performed, to be seen by an audience. In becoming part of the audience, we participate in and experience the drama collectively, enjoying the sensations of the story as a group. Indeed, participating in and being aware of that group dynamic is part of the experience of drama.

Differences in Engagement

Finally, drama and fiction tend to demand different approaches and responses. Fiction is usually narrated in the past tense. The fact that a narrator is recalling a story emphasises that these things have happened and that the narrative itself is a kind of reflection which involves judgments which are affected by a distance from events. In other words, the time between an occurrenec and the telling about it allows for a more informed reflection, narrative. The consequence of this, when put alongside the intimate nature of the reading experience, is that fiction is more contemplative.

Drama, however, is immediate and often more emotive. One reason for this is that, even if the stories are recalled, dialogue tends to be focused in the present tense, so it is as if the audience is witnessing the first unfolding of a story. In other words, drama does not have the sense of distance that fiction does: it attempts to engage an audience in the world of the characters in a more direct way. To some extent, this is what is meant when something is described as 'dramatic'; one means that it has an impact that involves the onlooker, grabs the attention and affects the viewer.

Key Terms and Glossary

KEY TERMS

PLOT

Plot refers to how the actions of a work are arranged in order to create a certain mood or emotional response. While a summary of a story outlines the incidents that occur, the plot involves an attempt to convey some sense of the overall atmosphere and what bearing the incidents have on a character.

SUB-PLOT

Sub-plots tend to be a feature of most dramas. A sub-plot involves the author taking different strands of the main plot and weaving them into a story with its own unity. A sub-plot tends to contribute to our understanding of the main plot by providing contrast, or by allowing the audience a greater insight into a character.

CONFLICT

Conflict is a term that suggests struggle. The struggle may be internal — a psychological struggle in which a character wrestles with the decisions he/she must make — or external — where there is a fight or an argument. However, conflict has to do with some kind of dis-ease.

TENSION

In drama, tension is a term that relates to the spark of discomfort or unease felt by characters in their relationships with each other. Tension is a term that refers to a mood they experience in response to their anxieties and concerns.

SUSPENSE

Suspense, a very important term when discussing drama, is used to describe an audience's anxiety about what may happen to characters with whom they have established some kind of bond. It is really a combination of curiosity (wanting to know what will happen in terms of story) and concern (a worry about the plight of the characters).

Suspense evolves from an interplay of audience involvement and distance. When an audience enters a theatre and watches a play, they suspend disbelief and enter into the world of the play. They become involved in the events taking place on stage, interested in watching the plot develop, wanting to know how the story develops. However, the audience are — by virtue of the fact that they are not actually part of the play itself — divorced from the action. They cannot influence its course, or change the lives the characters have been assigned. They must merely watch as the story unfolds. In other words, the audience are helpless observers, distanced from the action, who must wait to see what happens.

It is the tension between this involvement and distance that results in suspense — an atmosphere where the audience, who are concerned about the fate of the characters, must anxiously wait to see how the course of events will unfold.

SOLILOQUY

When a character is on stage alone and makes a speech, that speech is known as a soliloquy. The purpose of the soliloquy is to give the audience an insight into the true feelings and thoughts of the character, which sometimes may be different to the feelings that the character expresses to others on stage.

ASIDE

Asides, to some extent, have a similar function to soliloquies. An aside allows a character to make a comment on stage, while other characters are there, without the other characters hearing that remark. An aside, like the soliloquy, is a dramatic convention that allows the audience added perspective not available to other characters on stage.

COMIC RELIEF

In tragedy, comic relief is usually used to relieve tension and suspense at crucial times in the action. Comic relief makes use of humorous characters or comic situations to vary the play's rhythm, to allow the audience some release from the intensity of a scene, or to counterpoint and complement the main action.

CLIMAX AND ANTI-CLIMAX

When a piece of action or a scene reaches its high point and a resolution is required, the moment of decision, confrontation, or conflict leading to that resolution is referred to as a climax.

However, if the author decides to delay that climax having first allowed the audience to anticipate its arrival (for example, by switching from tragedy to comedy) then there is an anti-climax.

GLOSSARY

OXYMORON

Oxymoron is a form of metaphor, a kind of figure of speech in which contradictory elements are joined together. When Romeo says 'O loving hate' or 'O heavy lightness', and 'Feather of lead . . . cold fire', he is using *oxymorons*.

HYPERBOLE

Hyperbole is a kind of deliberate exaggeration which is not meant literally:

> The brightness of her cheek would shame those stars
> as daylight doth a lamp.

BLANK VERSE

Blank verse is when the lines of poetry lack end-line rhyme but have a definite rhythm pattern. In *Romeo and Juliet* Shakespeare uses iambic pentameter for most of his rhythms.

IAMBIC PENTAMETER

When lines of poetry consist of ten syllables which are divided into fine beats called *iambs*, that meter is called iambic pentameter. An *iamb* has a short sound (syllable) followed by a stressed one.

$$\overset{\vee}{\text{The}} \overset{-}{\text{time}} \mid \overset{\vee}{\text{and}} \overset{-}{\text{my}} \mid \overset{\vee}{\text{intents}} \overset{-}{} \mid \overset{\vee}{\text{are}} \overset{-}{\text{sav}} \mid \overset{\vee}{\text{age}} \overset{-}{\text{wild}}$$

This is the meter mostly used by Shakespeare in *Romeo and Juliet*.

The Most Excellent and Lamentable Tragedy of Romeo and Juliet

DRAMATIS PERSONÆ

ESCALUS, *Price of Verona.*
MERCUTIO, *a young gentleman and kinsman to the Prince, friend of Romeo.*
PARIS, *a noble young kinsman to the Prince.*
Page to Paris.

MONTAGUE, *head of a Veronese family at feud with the Capulets.*
LADY MONTAGUE.
ROMEO, *Montague's son.*
BENVOLIO, *Montague's nephew and friend of Romeo and Mercutio.*
ABRAM, *a servant to Montague.*
BALTHASAR, *Romeo's servant.*

CAPULET, *head of a Veronese family at feud with the Montauges.*
LADY CAPULET.
JULIET, *Capulet's daughter.*
TYBALT, *Lady Capulet's nephew.*
Capulet's Cousin, an old gentleman.
NURSE, *a Capulet servant, Juliet's foster-mother.*
PETER, *a Capulet servant attending on the Nurse.*
SAMPSON,
GREGORY,
ANTHONY, } *of the Capulet household.*
POTPAN,
SERVINGMEN,

FRIAR LAURENCE, } *of the Franciscan Order.*
FRIAR JOHN,
An Apothecary of Mantua.
Three Musicians (Simon Catling, Hugh Rebeck, James Soundpost).
Members of the Watch, Citizens of Verona, Masquers, Torchbearers, Pages, Servants.
CHORUS.

The Most Excellent and Lamentable Tragedy of Romeo and Juliet

THE PROLOGUE

vii   [*Enter* CHORUS.]

Chorus.   Two households both alike in dignity

     (In fair Verona, where we lay our scene)

     From ancient grudge break to new mutiny,

     Where civil blood makes civil hands unclean.

     From forth the fatal loins of these two foes   5

     A pair of star-cross'd lovers take their life,

     Whose misadventur'd piteous overthrows

     Doth with their death bury their parents' strife.

     The fearful passage of their death-mark'd love

     And the continuance of their parents' rage,   10

     Which, but their children's end, nought could remove,

     Is now the two hours' traffic of our stage;

     The which, if you with patient ears attend,

     What here shall miss, our toil shall strive to mend.

                                                  [*Exit.*]

[ACT I]
[SCENE I]

Introduction

This scene is set in a market place in Verona. Members of the Capulet household mock the Montagues. A street brawl develops that soon involves both young and old, disrupting the peace of the town and endangering the townspeople.

The Prince arrives and restores peace, warning the families that further feuding will result in death.

Romeo is noticeably absent from the fight. When Benvolio goes in search of him, he finds him pining for love.

Enter SAMPSON *and* GREGORY, *with swords and bucklers, of the house of Capulet.*

Samp.	Gregory, on my word we'll not carry coals.
Greg.	No, for then we should be colliers.
Samp.	I mean, and we be in choler, we'll draw.
Greg.	Ay, while you live, draw your neck out of collar.
Samp.	I strike quickly being moved. 5
Greg.	But thou art not quickly moved to strike.
Samp.	A dog of the house of Montague moves me.
Greg.	To move is to stir, and to be valiant is to stand: therefore if thou art moved thou runn'st away.
Samp.	A dog of that house shall move me to stand. I will 10 take the wall of any man or maid of Montague's.
Greg.	That shows thee a weak slave, for the weakest goes to the wall.
Samp.	'Tis true, and therefore women, being the weaker vessels, are ever thrust to the wall; therefore I will 15 push Montague's men from the wall, and thrust his maids to the wall.
Greg.	The quarrel is between our masters and us their men.

1 *not carry coals*
be insulted
2 *colliers*
dishonest
3 *in choler*
angry
4 *draw . . . collar*
avoid being
hanged

11 *take the wall*
be superior to

13 *goes to the wall*
loses

Samp.	'Tis all one. I will show myself a tyrant: when I have fought with the men I will be civil with the maids, I will cut off their heads.	20
Greg.	The heads of the maids?	
Samp.	Ay, the heads of the maids, or their maidenheads; take it in what sense thou wilt.	25
Greg.	They must take it in sense that feel it.	
Samp.	Me they shall feel while I am able to stand, and 'tis known I am a pretty piece of flesh.	
Greg.	'Tis well thou art not fish; if thou hadst, thou hadst been Poor John. Draw thy tool — here comes of the house of Montagues.	30

24 maidenheads
virginity

Enter two other Servingmen [ABRAM *and* BALTHASAR].

Samp.	My naked weapon is out. Quarrel, I will back thee.	
Greg.	How, turn thy back and run?	
Samp.	Fear me not.	35
Greg.	No, marry! I fear thee!	
Samp.	Let us take the law of our sides: let them begin.	
Greg.	I will frown as I pass by, and let them take it as they list.	
Samp.	Nay, as they dare. I will bite my thumb at them, which is disgrace to them if they bear it.	40
Abram.	Do you bite your thumb at us, sir?	
Samp.	I do bite my thumb, sir.	
Abram.	Do you bite your thumb at us, sir?	
Samp.	Is the law of our side if I say ay?	45
Greg.	No.	
Samp.	No sir, I do not bite my thumb at you, sir, but I bite my thumb, sir.	
Greg.	Do you quarrel, sir?	
Abram.	Quarrel, sir? No, sir.	50
Samp.	But if you do, sir, I am for you. I serve as good a man as you.	

37 of our sides
on our side

Abram.	No, better.	
Samp.	Well, sir.	

Enter BENVOLIO.

Greg.	Say 'better', here comes one of my master's	55
	kinsmen.	
Samp.	Yes, better, sir.	
Abram.	You lie.	
Samp.	Draw if you be men. Gregory, remember thy	
	washing blow. *They fight.*	60
Ben.	Part, fools, put up your swords, you know not what	
	you do.	

60 *washing*
slashing

Enter TYBALT.

Tyb.	What, art thou drawn among these heartless hinds?	
	Turn thee, Benvolio, look upon thy death.	
Ben.	I do but keep the peace, put up thy sword,	65
	Or manage it to part these men with me.	
Tyb.	What, drawn, and talk of peace? I hate the word,	
	As I hate hell, all Montagues, and thee:	
	Have at thee, coward. *[They] fight.*	

63 *heartless hinds*
cowardly
servants

Enter three or four Citizens *with clubs or partisans.*

Citizens.	Clubs, bills and partisans! Strike! Beat them	70
	down! Down with the Capulets! Down with the	
	Montagues!	

70 *partisans*
spears

Enter old CAPULET *in his gown, and* LADY CAPULET.

Cap.	What noise is this? Give me my long sword, ho!
Lady Cap.	A crutch, a crutch! Why call you for a sword?

Enter old MONTAGUE *and* LADY MONTAGUE.

Cap.   My sword I say! Old Montague is come,   75
       And flourishes his blade in spite of me.

Mont. Thou villain Capulet! Hold me not! Let me go!

Lady Mont. Thou shalt not stir one foot to seek a foe

Prince.   *Throw your mistemper'd weapons to the ground*
               And hear the sentence of your moved Prince.   lines 85–6

       Enter Prince ESCALUS *with his* TRAIN.

Prince.   Rebellious subjects, enemies to peace,
          Profaners of this neighbour-stained steel —   80
          Will they not hear? What ho! You men, you beasts!
          That quench the fire of your pernicious rage
          With purple fountains issuing from your veins,
          On pain of torture from those bloody hands
          Throw your mistemper'd weapons to the ground   85
          And hear the sentence of your moved prince.
          Three civil brawls bred of an airy word
          By thee, old Capulet, and Montague,
          Have thrice disturb'd the quiet of our streets

	And made Verona's ancient citizens	90
	Cast by their grave-beseeming ornaments	
	To wield old partisans, in hands as old,	
	Canker'd with peace, to part your canker'd hate.	
	If ever you disturb our streets again	
	Your lives shall pay the forfeit of the peace.	95

93 *Canker'd
. . . canker'd*
rusted
. . . malignant

And made Verona's ancient citizens 90
Cast by their grave-beseeming ornaments
To wield old partisans, in hands as old,
Canker'd with peace, to part your canker'd hate.
If ever you disturb our streets again
Your lives shall pay the forfeit of the peace. 95
For this time all the rest depart away;
You, Capulet, shall go along with me,
And Montague, come you this afternoon,
To know our farther pleasure in this case,
To old Freetown, our common judgement-place. 100
Once more, on pain of death, all men depart.

Exeunt [all but Montague, Lady Montague and Benvolio].

Mont. Who set this ancient quarrel new abroach?
Speak, nephew, were you by when it began?

Ben. Here were the servants of your adversary
And yours, close fighting ere I did approach. 105
I drew to part them; in the instant came
The fiery Tybalt, with his sword prepar'd,
Which, as he breath'd defiance to my ears
He swung about his head and cut the winds,
Who nothing hurt withal, hiss'd him in scorn. 110
While we were interchanging thrusts and blows
Came more and more, and fought on part and part,
Till the Prince came, who parted either part.

Lady Mont. O where is Romeo, saw you him today?
Right glad I am he was not at this fray. 115

Ben. Madam, an hour before the worshipp'd sun
Peer'd forth the golden window of the east
A troubled mind drive me to walk abroad,
Where underneath the grove of sycamore
That westward rooteth from this city side 120
So early walking did I see your son.
Towards him I made, but he was ware of me,
And stole into the covert of the wood.
I, measuring his affections by my own,

102 *new abroach*
newly open

	Which then most sought, where most might not be found,	125
	Being one too many by my weary self,	
	Pursu'd my humour, not pursuing his,	
	And gladly shunn'd who gladly fled from me.	
Mont.	Many a morning hath he there been seen,	
	With tears augmenting the fresh morning's dew,	130
	Adding to clouds more clouds with his deep sighs;	
	But all so soon as the all-cheering sun	
	Should in the farthest east begin to draw	
	The shady curtains from Aurora's bed,	
	Away from light steals home my heavy son	135
	And private in his chamber pens himself,	
	Shuts up his windows, locks fair daylight out	
	And makes himself an artificial night.	
	Black and portentous must this humour prove	
	Unless good counsel may the cause remove.	140
Ben.	My noble uncle, do you know the cause?	
Mont.	I neither know it nor can learn of him.	
Ben.	Have you importun'd him by any means?	
Mont.	Both by myself and many other friends.	
	But he, his own affections' counsellor,	145
	Is to himself — I will not say how true —	
	But to himself so secret and so close,	
	So far from sounding and discovery,	
	As is the bud bit with an envious worm	
	Ere he can spread his sweet leaves to the air	150
	Or dedicate his beauty to the sun.	
	Could we but learn from whence his sorrows grow,	
	We would as willingly give cure as know.	

134 *Aurora* Goddess of the dawn

135 *heavy* sad

139 *portentous* ominous

143 *importun'd* asked

Enter ROMEO.

Ben.	See where he comes. So please you step aside;	
	I'll know his grievance or be much denied.	155
Mont.	I would thou wert so happy by thy stay	

To hear true shrift. Come, madam, let's away.

Exeunt [Montague and Lady Montague].

Ben.   Good morrow, cousin.

Romeo.   Is the day so young?

Ben.   But new struck nine.

Romeo.   Ay me, sad hours seem long.

Was that my father that went hence so fast?   160

Ben.   It was. What sadness lengthens Romeo's hours?

Romeo.   Not having that which, having, makes them short.

Ben.   In love?

Romeo.   Out.

Ben.   Of love?   165

Romeo.   Out of her favour where I am in love.

Ben.   Alas that love so gentle in his view

Should be so tyrannous and rough in proof.

Romeo.   Alas that love whose view is muffled still

Should without eyes see pathways to his will.   170

Where shall we dine? O me! What fray was here?

Yet tell me not, for I have heard it all.

Here's much to do with hate, but more with love.

Why then, O brawling love, O loving hate,

O anything of nothing first create!   175

O heavy lightness, serious vanity,

Misshapen chaos of well-seeming forms!

Feather of lead, bright smoke, cold fire, sick health,

Still-waking sleep that is not what it is!

This love feel I that feel no love in this.   180

Dost thou not laugh?

Ben.   No coz, I rather weep.

Romeo.   Good heart, at what?

Ben.   At thy good heart's oppression.

Romeo.   Why such is love's transgression.

Griefs of mine own lie heavy in my breast,

Which thou wilt propagate to have it press'd   185

With more of thine. This love that thou hast shown

Doth add more grief to too much of mine own.

168 *in proof* inexperience

169–170 *Alas that love . . . to his will.* Alas, that Cupid causes people to fall in love.

177 *well-seeming forms* beautiful things

179 *Still-waking sleep* sleeplessness

181 *coz* cousin

183 *transgression* disadvantage

185 *propagate* increase

Love is a smoke made with the fume of sighs;

Being purg'd, a fire sparkling in lovers' eyes;

Being vexed, a sea nourish'd with lovers' tears; 190

What is it else? A madness most discreet,

A choking gall, and a preserving sweet.

Farewell, my coz.

Ben.   Soft, I will go along;

And if you leave me so, you do me wrong.

Romeo. Tut, I have lost myself, I am not here. 195

This is not Romeo, he's some other where.

Ben. Tell me in sadness who is that you love?

Romeo. What, shall I groan and tell thee?

Ben. Groan? Why no, but sadly tell me who.

Romeo. Bid a sick man in sadness make his will? 200

A word ill-urg'd to one that is so ill.

In sadness, cousin, I do love a woman.

Ben. I aim'd so near when I suppos'd you lov'd.

Romeo. A right good markman; and she's fair I love.

Ben. A right fair mark, fair coz, is soonest hit. 205

Romeo. Well, in that hit you miss; she'll not be hit

With Cupid's arrow, she hath Dian's wit,

And in strong proof of chastity well arm'd

From love's weak childish bow she lives uncharm'd.

She will not stay the siege of loving terms 210

Nor bide th'encounter of assailing eyes

Nor ope her lap to saint-seducing gold;

O she is rich in beauty, only poor

That when she dies, with beauty dies her store.

Ben. Then she hath sworn that she will still live chaste? 215

Romeo. She hath, and in that sparing makes huge waste.

For beauty starv'd with her severity

Cuts beauty off from all posterity.

She is too fair, too wise, wisely too fair,

To merit bliss by making me despair. 220

She hath forsworn to love, and in that vow

Do I live dead, that live to tell it now.

189 *purg'd*
cleansed

192 *choking gall*
choking bitterness

193 *Soft*
wait a minute

197 *in sadness*
seriously

207 *Dian'*
Diana, goddess
of chastity

214 *dies her store*
she won't have
children

221 *forsworn to*
sworn not to

Ben.	Be rul'd by me, forget to think of her.	
Romeo.	O teach me how I should forget to think.	
Ben.	By giving liberty unto thine eyes:	225
	Examine other beauties.	
Romeo.	'Tis the way.	
	To call hers, exquisite, in question more	
	These happy masks that kiss fair ladies' brows,	
	Being black, puts us in mind they hide the fair.	
	He that is strucken blind cannot forget	230
	The precious treasure of his eyesight lost.	
	Show me a mistress that is passing fair;	
	What doth her beauty serve but as a note	
	Where I may read who pass'd that passing fair?	
	Farewell, thou canst not teach me to forget.	235
Ben.	I'll pay that doctrine or else die in debt.	*Exeunt.*

SCENE ANALYSIS

ACTION

1. Capulet servants mock Montague servants.
2. A brawl develops on the streets of Verona.
3. Young and old from both houses are involved.
4. Tybalt jeers Benvolio's efforts to halt the fight.
5. Prince Escalus warns that another fight will be punishable by death.
6. Romeo is absent from the action.
7. Benvolio and the Montagues discuss Romeo's moodiness.
8. Romeo explains to Benvolio that he is in love but that his love is not returned. Benvolio tells him to forget the woman.

THEMES

1. The feud opens the play. The hatred between the families is evident.
2. The second half of the scene introduces the theme of love, which is then contrasted with that of hate.

CHARACTERISATION

1. The servants, Sampson and Gregory, are crude and vulgar in their language and behaviour.

2. Benvolio emerges as a reasonable young man who wishes to avoid conflict.

3. Tybalt is a dangerous character who delights in confrontation. He is an expert swordsman who is feared by all. He is an agent of suspense within the play. He hates peace.

4. Romeo is lovesick, melancholy and courtly. He is playing the role of courtly lover whose love is unrequited.

DRAMATIC EFFECT/CONTENT

1. The scene is filled with movement and life.

2. It has lots of colour and is crowded with characters.

3. It establishes the play as a drama about youth.

4. There is conflict and suspense.

5. The scene has much humour but also violence, the spirits of life and death.

6. The plot is introduced immediately. The Prince threatens anyone who may disturb the peace. The characters will live under the threat of this edict.

LANGUAGE

1. The servants' language is littered with vulgar metaphors, indicating their common nature.

2. The language of the shorter exchanges tends towards prose, while that of the longer exchanges are poetry, but in blank verse.

3. Romeo speaks in rhymes. His speech is mannered and stylised. This draws attention to him being in love with the idea of love rather than with Rosaline. He gives many definitions of love, but they tend to be conventional views, suggesting that he plays the role of courtly lover.

[SCENE II]

Introduction

This is a transition scene which has two sections. First, the scene involves a conversation with Capulet and Paris, a young nobleman who wishes to marry Juliet. Capulet tells Paris that his daughter is only thirteen. However, he invites Paris to a feast he is giving and asks him to woo her there.

Romeo and Benvolio then enter the scene and meet Capulet's servant. They read the guest list for the feast and decide to attend it themselves.

Enter CAPULET, PARIS *and a* Servant.

Cap.	But Montague is bound as well as I,	1 *is bound as well* sworn to peace
	In penalty alike and 'tis not hard I think	
	For men so old as we to keep the peace.	
Paris.	Of honourable reckoning are you both,	4 *honourable reckoning* good reputation
	And pity 'tis you lived at odds so long	5
	But now my lord, what say you to my suit?	
Cap.	But saying o'er what I have said before.	
	My child is yet a stranger in the world,	
	She hath not seen the change of fourteen years.	
	Let two more summers wither in their pride	10
	Ere we may think her ripe to be a bride.	
Paris.	Younger than she are happy mothers made.	
Cap.	And too soon marr'd are those so early made.	
	Earth hath swallow'd all my hopes but she;	
	She is the hopeful lady of my earth.	15
	But woo her, gentle Paris, get her heart,	
	My will to her consent is but a part,	
	And she agreed, within her scope of choice	
	Lies my consent and fair according voice.	
	This night I hold an old accustom'd feast	20
	Whereto I have invited many a guest	
	Such as I love and you among the store:	
	One more, most welcome, makes my number more.	

At my poor house look to behold this night

Earth-treading stars that make dark heaven light.   25

Such comfort as do lusty young men feel

When well-apparell'd April on the heel

Of limping winter treads, even such delight

Among fresh female buds shall you this night

Inherit at my house. Hear all, all see,   30

And like her most whose merit most shall be;

Which, on more view of many, mine, being one,

May stand in number, though in reckoning none.

Come go with me. [*To servant.*] Go sirrah, trudge about

Through fair Verona, find those persons out   35

Whose names are written there, and to them say,

My house and welcome on their pleasure stay.

                    [*Exeunt [Capulet and Paris]*].

Ser.   Find them out whose manes are written here. It is

written that the shoemaker should meddle with his

yard, and the tailor with his last, the fisher with his   40

pencil, and the painter with his nets, but I am sent

to find those persons whose names are here writ, and

can never find what names the writing person hath

here writ. I must to the learned. In good time.

Enter BENVOLIO *and* ROMEO.

Ben.   Tut man, one fire burns out another's burning,   45

          One pain is lessen'd by another's anguish;

          Turn giddy, and be holp by backward turning.

          One desperate grief cures with another's languish;

          Take thou some new infection to thy eye

          And the rank poison of the old will die.   50

Romeo.   Your plantain leaf is excellent for that.

Ben.   For what, I pray thee?

Romeo.   For your broken shin.

Ben.   Why, Romeo, art thou mad?

Romeo.   Not mad, but bound more than a madman is:

25 Earth-treading stars
beautiful women

37 stay
await

47 be holp
be helped
*48–50 One
desperate . . . will
die.*
One love becomes
a cure for another.
49 new infection
new love interest
51 plantain leaf
dockleaf, cure

13

	Shut up in prison, kept without my food,	55
	Whipp'd and tormented and — good e'en, good fellow.	
Ser.	God gi' good e'en; I pray sir, can you read?	
Romeo.	Ay, mine own fortune in my misery.	
Ser.	Perhaps you have learned it without book. But I pray	
	can you read anything you see?	60
Romeo.	Ay, if I know the letters and the language.	
Ser.	Ye say honestly; rest you merry.	
Romeo.	Stay, fellow, I can read	*He reads the letter.*

Signor Martino and his wife and daughters;

Count Anselm and his beauteous sisters;   65

The lady widow of Utruvio;

Signor Placentio and his lovely nieces;

Mercutio and his brother Valentine;

Mine uncle Capulet, his wife and daughters;

My fair niece Rosaline and Livia;   70

Signor Valentio and his cousin Tybalt;

Lucio and the lively Helena.

	A fair assembly. Whither should they come?	
Ser.	Up.	
Romeo.	Whither to supper?	75
Ser.	To our house.	
Romeo.	Whose house?	
Ser.	My master's.	
Romeo.	Indeed I should have asked you that before.	
Ser.	Now I'll tell you without asking. My master is the	80
	great rich Capulet, and if you be not of the house of	
	Montagues I pray come and crush a cup of wine.	
	Rest you merry.	*Exit*
Ben.	At this same ancient feast of Capulet's	
Sups	the fair Rosaline, whom thou so loves,	85
	With all the admired beauties of Verona.	
	Go thither and with unattainted eye	
	Compare her face with some that I shall show	
	And I will make thee think thy swan a crow.	
Romeo.	When the devout religion of mine eye	90

56 *good e'en*
good evening

Maintains such falsehood, then turn tears to fire,
And these who, often drown'd, could never die,
Transparent heretics, be burnt for liars.

93 Transparent heretics obvious disbelievers

One fairer than my love! The all-seeing sun
Ne'er saw her match since first the world begun.   95

Ben. Tut, you saw her fair, none else being by:
Herself pois'd with herself in either eye.
But in that crystal scales let there be weigh'd

98 crystal scales Romeo's eyes

Your lady's love against some other maid
That I will show you shining at this feast,   100
And she shall scant show well that now seems best.

101 shall scant show well scarcely seem attractive

Romeo. I'll go along, so such sight to be shown,
But to rejoice in splendour of mine own.   [*Exeunt.*]

103 splendour of mine own Rosaline

SCENE ANALYSIS

ACTION

1. Capulet tells Paris, a cousin of Prince Escalus, that the Prince's warning about future disturbances applies also to the Montagues and that it should not be hard for 'men so old as we to keep the peace'.
2. Paris asks Capulet to consider his suit of marriage to Juliet.
3. Capulet asks Paris to be patient, telling him that Juliet is still only thirteen and requests that he wait 'two more summers' before marrying her.
4. He invites Paris to his feast where he can try to win Juliet's consent.
5. He sends a servant to invite the people whose names are written on a list to the feast. However, the servant cannot read.
6. Romeo and Benvolio meet the servant and read the list for him.
7. Benvolio suggests that they go to the party where Romeo will see Rosaline and Benvolio will cure him of his infatuation: 'I will make thee think thy swan a crow'.

THEMES

1. Once again there is a reference to the feud at the opening of the scene, with Paris' comment

    > Of honourable reckoning are you both;
    > And pity 'tis you lived at odds so long,

    drawing attention to the pointlessness of the feud. Furthermore, when talking to Romeo and Benvolio, the servant tells them that they are welcome to the feast as long as they are not of the house of Montague.
2. The theme of the different generations is introduced when Capulet says that men as old as he and Montague should be able to keep the peace.
3. The idea of love as a contract is also introduced as a theme in this scene. Paris approaches Capulet to ask for Juliet's hand in marriage. He appears to have no genuine feelings for Juliet, but is looking for an arranged marriage: that is, he wants Juliet's father to give Juliet to him.
4. Romeo's love for Rosaline is once more mentioned, contrasting the theme of courtly love with the contractual approach to marriage taken by Paris.

CHARACTERISATION

1. Capulet appears to be a reasonable man. He seems to want peace and obviously loves his daughter:

    > Earth hath swallowed all my hopes but she,
    > She is the hopeful lady of my earth.

    He doesn't want to lose her to a husband quite yet and asks Paris to delay awhile. He also advises Paris to woo Juliet:

    > . . . get her heart,
    > My will to her consent is but a part,

    in the hope that the marriage will be built on affection.
2. Paris seems to be an earnest young man. He regrets the fact that there is a feud between the Capulet and Montague families. His intentions in wanting to marry Juliet seem honourable, although they are not based on love. He is quite determined to have her as his bride — 'Younger than she are happy mothers made'. He is respected and is a nobleman, related to Prince Escalus.

3. Romeo would like to be faithful in love. He responds to Benvolio's taunts about Rosaline with an insistence that he loves only her. He comes across as sincere, if a little naïve.

DRAMATIC EFFECT

1. The scene reminds the audience that the Prince has put an order in place that will govern the lives of the characters.
2. The plot develops in terms of complexity with the introduction of Paris and his proposal to marry Juliet.
3. The scene is humorous in the section where the servant is unable to read and in Benvolio's teasing of Romeo.

LANGUAGE

1. Initially the language of Capulet and Paris is prosaic, but, when talking of his daughter, Capulet's language becomes poetic. He uses figures of speech when describing the upcoming feast, conjuring up an image of a wonderful banquet which will provide a setting for love.
2. Romeo's language when talking of Rosaline contains the metaphor of religious faith to describe love.
3. The language of the servant contrasts with the speech of others in the scene: his language is uneducated and prosaic, literal and lacking refinement, indicating his low social rank.

[SCENE III]

Introduction

Juliet is introduced in this scene. Lady Capulet raises the topic of marriage with her daughter and asks her to consider Paris, who will be attending the feast, as a prospective suitor. She is helped and hindered in her efforts to discuss the topic by the Nurse who has been Juliet's guardian and Nanny.

Enter LADY CAPULET *and* NURSE.

Lady Cap.   Nurse, where's my daughter? Call her forth to me.

Nurse.	Now by my maidenhead at twelve year old,
	I bade her come. What, lamb. What, ladybird.
	God forbid. Where's this girl? What, Juliet!

Enter JULIET.

Juliet.	How now, who calls?	
Nurse.	Your mother.	5
Juliet.	Madam, I am here, what is your will?	
Lady Cap.	This is the matter. Nurse, give leave awhile,	
	We must talk in secret. Nurse, come back again,	
	I have remember'd me, thou's hear our counsel.	
	Thou knowest my daughter's of a pretty age.	10
Nurse.	Faith, I can tell her age unto an hour.	
Lady Cap.	She's not fourteen.	
Nurse.	I'll lay fourteen of my teeth —	
	And yet, to my teen be it spoken, I have but four —	
	She's not fourteen. How long is it now	
	To Lammas-tide?	
Lady Cap.	A fortnight and odd days.	15
Nurse.	Even or odd, of all days in the year,	
	Come Lammas Eve at night shall she be fourteen.	
	Susan and she — God rest all Christian souls —	
	Were of an age. Well, Susan is with God;	
	She was too good for me. But as I said,	20
	On Lammas Eve at night shall she be fourteen.	
	That shall she; marry, I remember it well.	
	'Tis since the earthquake now eleven years,	
	And she was wean'd — I never shall forget it —	
	Of all the days of the year upon that day.	25
	For I had then laid wormwood to my dug,	
	Sitting in the sun under the dovehouse wall.	
	My lord and you were then at Mantua —	
	Nay I do bear a brain. But as I said,	
	When it did taste the wormwood on the nipple	30
	Of my dug and felt it bitter, pretty fool,	

13 *to my teen*
o my sorrow

17 *Lammas Eve*
August 1st

26 *wormwood★ to*
my dug★
a bitter herb★ put
to the breast★ to
stop the baby
taking mother's
milk

29 *bear a brain*
have a good
memory

To see it tetchy and fall out with the dug.

Shake! quoth the dovehouse. 'Twas no need, I trow,

To bid me trudge.

And since that time it is eleven years.   35

For then she could stand high-lone, nay, by th'rood,

She could have run and waddled all about;

For even the day before she broke her brow,

And then my husband — God be with his soul,

A was a merry man — took up the child,   40

'Yea', quoth he, 'dost thou fall upon thy face?

Thou wilt fall backward when thou hast more wit,

Wilt thou not, Jule?' And by my holidame,

The pretty wretch left crying and said 'Ay'.

To see now how a jest shall come about.   45

I warrant, and I should live a thousand years

I never should forget it. 'Wilt thou not, Jule?' quoth he,

And, pretty fool, it stinted, and said 'Ay'.

Lady Cap. Enough of this, I pray thee, hold thy peace.

Nurse.   Yes madam, yet I cannot choose but laugh   50

To think it should leave crying and say 'Ay';

And yet I warrant it had upon it brow

A bump as big as a young cockerel's stone,

A perilous knock, and it cried bitterly.

'Yea', quoth my husband, 'fall'st upon thy face?   55

Thou wilt fall backward when thou comest to age,

Wilt thou not, Jule?' It stinted, and said 'Ay'.

Juliet.   And stint thou too, I pray thee, Nurse, say I.

Nurse.   Peace, I have done. God mark thee to his grace,

Thou wast the prettiest babe that e'er I nurs'd.   60

And I might live to see thee married once,

I have my wish.

Lady Cap. Marry, that marry is the very theme

I came to talk of. Tell me, daughter Juliet,

How stands your dispositions to be married?   65

Juliet.   It is an honour that I dream not of.

32 *tetchy*
peevish, irritable

36 *th'rood*
the cross

63 *Marry*
By Mary

19

Lady Capulet. . . . *Tell me, daughter Juliet*
How stands your dispositions to be married? lines 64–5

Nurse.	An honour. Were not I thine only nurse
	I would say thou hadst suck'd wisdom from thy teat.
Lady Cap.	Well, think of marriage now. Younger than you
	Here in Verona, ladies of esteem, 70
	Are made already mothers. By my count
	I was your mother much upon these years
	That you are now a maid. Thus then in brief:
	The valiant Paris seeks you for his love.
Nurse.	A man, young lady. Lady, such a man 75
	As all the world — why, he's a man of wax.
Lady Cap.	Verona's summer hath not such a flower.
Nurse.	Nay, he's a flower, in faith a very flower.
Lady Cap.	What say you, can you love the gentleman?
	This night you shall behold him at our feast; 80
	Read o'er the volume of young Paris' face
	And find delight writ there with beauty's pen.
	Examine every married lineament
	And see how one another lends content;
	And what obscur'd in this fair volume lies, 85
	Find written in the margent of his eyes.
	This precious book of love, this unbound lover,
	To beautify him only lacks a cover.

Side notes:

76 *a man of wax*
a perfect man

83 *married*
lineament
well balanced part

84 *one another lends*
content
one complements
another

86 *margent*
margin

The fish lives in the sea; and 'tis much pride

For fair without the fair within to hide.   90

That book in many's eyes doth share the glory

That in gold clasps locks in the golden story.

So shall you share all that he doth possess,

By having him, making yourself no less.

Nurse. No less, nay bigger. Women grow by men.   95

Lady Cap. Speak briefly, can you like of Paris' love?

Juliet. I'll look to like, if looking liking move,

But no more deep will I endart mine eye

Than your consent gives strength to make it fly.

Enter a Servingman.

Ser. Madam, the guests are come, supper served up, you   100

called, my young lady asked for, the Nurse cursed in

the pantry, and everything in extremity. I must

hence to wait, I beseech you follow straight.   *Exit.*   103 *to wait*
to serve guests

Lady Cap. We follow thee; Juliet, the County stays.

Nurse. Go, girl, seek happy nights to happy days.   105

Exeunt.

SCENE ANALYSIS

ACTION

1. Lady Capulet sends for Juliet to talk to her about marriage.
2. The Nurse says that Juliet will soon be fourteen, remembering that it is eleven years since the earthquake. Her own daughter, Susan, died and she and Juliet would have been the same age.
3. Juliet's mother introduces the topic of marriage and informs her daughter that Paris wishes to marry her.
4. Juliet says that she will do what her mother wishes and that she will go along to the feast and see what Paris is like.

THEMES

1. The theme of love is, once again, the main subject of discussion. Here the topic is the prospect of an arranged marriage — a marriage in terms of a contract or a social obligation. In contrast to this the Nurse's view of love tends to focus merely on the physical:

   > . . . fall'st upon thy face?
   > Thou wilt fall backward when thou comest to age . . .

   > Go, girl, seek happy nights to happy days.

2. The theme of the differences between the generations is indirectly referred to with the references to time.

CHARACTERISATION

1. Lady Capulet appears more pragmatic than her husband. She recognises Paris as a good match for her daughter: she describes him as 'valiant Paris', 'a precious book of love', 'Verona's summer hath not such a flower', an attempt to encourage her daughter to give her consent to such a match. We see that her relationship with Juliet seems to lack a certain intimacy, as she initially hesitates in bringing up the topic of marriage and requires the Nurse's presence for support.
2. Juliet is portrayed as a young and obedient girl who is willing to abide by the wishes of her parents: she says

   > But no more deep will I endart mine eye
   > Than your consent gives strength to make it fly.

3. The Nurse is a garrulous individual who likes to be involved in conversation. The fact that she is a servant is made apparent by her common behaviour and in the way that Lady Capulet has, more than once, to ask her to be quiet. Yet she appears to be close to Juliet and her anecdotes indicate her long service with the family.

DRAMATIC EFFECT

1. This is a scene with humour and gossip, a domestic scene that is intimate in mood.
2. It introduces the heroine of the play to the audience. As she has already been described by her father and a nobleman is seeking her hand in marriage, the audience is interested in finding out what she is like.

LANGUAGE

1. The language of Lady Capulet when describing Paris tends towards hyperbole (exaggeration), as she is intent on conveying a good impression of him to her daughter.

2. The Nurse speaks in prose, like the other servants in the play. Her language is crude and her humour tends to be bawdy: 'women grow by men', she says, which has vulgar connotations.

3. Juliet's language tends to be polite and formal, indicating her respect for her mother.

[SCENE IV]

Introduction

In this scene Romeo tells his companions, on their way to the Capulet masque feast, that he will observe, not participate. He also says that a dream he had suggests that attending the masque may bring bad luck. His friend, Mercutio, makes fun of this and gives a brilliant speech on the nature of dreams.

Enter ROMEO, MERCUTIO, BENVOLIO, *with five or six other*
MASQUERS [*and*] Torchbearers.

Romeo.	What, shall this speech be spoke for our excuse?		1 *speech* speech of apology
	Or shall we on without apology?		3 *is out* no longer fashionable
Ben.	The date is out of such prolixity.		
	We'll have no Cupid hoodwink'd with a scarf,		5 *painted bow of lath* an imitation bow
	Bearing a Tartar's painted bow of lath,	5	
	Scaring the ladies like a crowkeeper,		6 *a crowkeeper* boy dressed as a scarecrow
	Nor no without-book prologue, faintly spoke		
	After the prompter, for our entrance.		
	But let them measure us by what they will,		10 *measure them a measure* dance a slow dance
	We'll measure them a measure and be gone.	10	
Romeo.	Give me a torch, I am not for this ambling.		11 *ambling* dancing
	Being but heavy I will bear the light.		

Mer.	Nay, gentle Romeo, we must have you dance.	
Romeo.	Not I, believe me. You have dancing shoes	
	With nimble soles, I have a soul of lead	15
	So stakes me to the ground I cannot move.	
Mer.	You are a lover, borrow Cupid's wings	
	And soar with them above a common bound.	
Romeo.	I am too sore enpierced with his shaft	
	To soar with his light feathers, and so bound	20
	I cannot bound a pitch above dull woe.	
	Under love's heavy burden do I sink.	
Mer.	And, to sink in it, should you burden love —	
	Too great oppression for a tender thing.	
Romeo.	Is love a tender thing? It is too rough,	25
	Too rude, too boisterous, and it pricks like thorn.	
Mer.	If love be rough with you, be rough with love;	
	Prick love for pricking and you beat love down.	
	Give me a case to put my visage in:	
	A visor for a visor. What care I	30
	What curious eye doth quote deformities?	
	Here are the beetle brows shall blush for me.	
Ben.	Come, knock and enter, and no sooner in	
	But every man betake him to his legs.	
Romeo.	A torch for me. Let wantons light of heart	35
	Tickle the senseless rushes with their heels,	
	For I am proverb'd with a grandsire phrase —	
	I'll be a candle-holder and look on.	
	The game was ne'er so fair, and I am done.	
Mer.	Tut, dun's the mouse, the constable's own word.	40
	If thou art dun, we'll draw thee from the mire	
	Of — save your reverence — love, wherein thou stickest	
	Up to the ears. Come, we burn daylight, ho.	
Romeo.	Nay, that's not so.	
Mer.	I mean sir, in delay	
	We waste our lights in vain, light lights by day.	45
	Take our good meaning, for our judgement sits	
	Five times in that ere once in our five wits.	

21 *pitch* height

29 *visage* mask

30 *visor for a visor* putting a mask on a face which is like a mask

32 *beetle brows shall blush* bushy eyebrows and red cheeks on the mask

36 *senseless rushes* floor covering

37 *grandsire phrase* old man's proverb

39 *the game . . . fair* the proverb recommended quitting the game when it was at its best

40 *dun's the mouse* keep quiet

41 *dun* a stick in the mud

42 *save your reverence* excuse me (Mercutio is using a pun on 'sirreverence', slang for dung.)

43 *burn daylight* waste time

Romeo.	And we mean well in going to this masque,	
	But 'tis no wit to go.	
Mer.	Why, may one ask?	
Romeo.	I dreamt a dream tonight.	
Mer.	And so did I.	50
Romeo.	Well what was yours?	
Mer.	That dreamers often lie.	
Romeo.	In bed asleep, while they do dream things true.	
Mer.	O then I see Queen Mab hath been with you.	

She is the fairies' midwife, and she comes
In shape no bigger than an agate stone   55
On the forefinger of an alderman,
Drawn with a team of little atomi
Over men's noses as they lie asleep.
Her chariot is an empty hazelnut
Made by the joiner squirrel or old grub,   60
Time out o' mind the fairies' coachmakers;
Her waggon-spokes made of long spinners' legs,
The cover of the wings of grasshoppers,
Her traces of the smallest spider web,
Her collars of the moonshine's watery beams,   65
Her whip of cricket's bone, the lash of film,
Her waggoner a small grey-coated gnat,
Not half so big as a round little worm
Prick'd from the lazy finger of a maid;
And in this state she gallops night by night   70
Through lovers' brains, and then they dream of love;
O'er courtiers' knees, that dream on curtsies straight;
O'er lawyers' fingers who straight dream on fees;
O'er ladies' lips, who straight on kisses dream,
Which oft the angry Mab with blisters plagues   75
Because their breaths with sweetmeats tainted are.
Sometime she gallops o'er a courtier's nose
And then dreams he of smelling out a suit;
And sometime comes she with a tithe-pig's tail,
Tickling a parson's nose as a lies asleep;   80

57 *atomi*
small beings

62 *spinners*
spiders

78 *a suit*
a favour

79 *a tithe-pig's tail*
a pig given as a
part of taxes

25

Mercutio.   *True, I talk of dreams,*
Which are the children of an idle brain,
Begot of nothing but vain fantasy . . .   *lines 96–8*

Then dreams he of another benefice.
Sometimes she driveth o'er a soldier's neck
And then dreams he of cutting foreign throats,
Of breaches, ambuscados, Spanish blades,   84 *ambuscados*
Of healths five fathom deep; and then anon   85   ambushs
Drums in his ear, at which he starts and wakes,   85 *healths*
And being thus frighted swears a prayer or two   toasts to health
And sleeps again. This is that very Mab
That plaits the manes of horses in the night
And bakes the elf-locks in foul sluttish hairs,   90   90 *elf-locks*
Which, once untangled, much misfortune bodes.   dirty hair was
This is the hag, when maids lie on their backs,   regarded as the
That presses them and learns them first to bear,   work of elves
Making them women of good carriage.
This is she —
Romeo.   Peace, peace, Mercutio, peace.   95
Thou talk'st of nothing.
Mer.   True, I talk of dreams,
Which are the children of an idle brain,
Begot of nothing but vain fantasy,

Which is as thin of substance as the air

And more inconstant than the wind, who woos   100

Even now the frozen bosom of the north

And, being anger'd, puffs away from thence

Turning his side to the dew-dropping south.

Ben.   This wind you talk of blows us from ourselves:

Supper is done and we shall come too late.   105

Romeo.   I fear too early, for my mind misgives

Some consequence yet hanging in the stars

Shall bitterly begin his fearful date   108 *date*

With this night's revels, and expire the term   season

Of a despised life clos'd in my breast   110

By some vile forfeit of untimely death.

But he that hath the steerage of my course

Direct my suit. On, lusty gentlemen.

Ben.   Strike, drum.

SCENE ANALYSIS

ACTION

1. Romeo, Benvolio, Mercutio and five or six others are making their way to the Capulet home to attend the dance that follows the dinner. Unannounced masquers at such functions were natural enough in Shakespeare's day.

2. Romeo wonders what excuse they will use, but Benvolio says they will just enter, dance and leave.

3. However, Romeo is still reluctant and says that he will be a torchbearer. Mercutio insists that he must enter the spirit of the party and dance. He tells Romeo to be rough with love.

4. Romeo then says he had a dream, inspiring Mercutio to tease his friend with his speech about Queen Mab, 'the fairies midwife', who is responsible for all the dreams people have, 'dreams/Which are the children of an idle brain'.

5. Benvolio tells Mercutio that his ramblings will make them late for the dance.

6. Romeo has a sense of foreboding. He feels that Fate, 'Some consequence yet hanging in the stars', has marked this night as the beginning of something that will

result in his death. He puts his own faith in the powers that guide his destiny, asking for their 'steerage of my course'.

CHARACTERISATION

1. Mercutio is a lively and witty character who enjoys banter and who constantly seeks to put Romeo in good humour. He has a cynical attitude to love, rather like the Nurse, and he advises Romeo not to take love seriously:

> If love be rough with you, be rough with love;
> Prick love for pricking and you beat love down.

His Queen Mab speech is a marvel of imagination and clarity, connecting everything through association of ideas.

2. Romeo would like to be as joyful as his friends, but is still melancholic due to his doting on Rosaline. He is reluctant to go to the masque because he is not in the humour and because he had a dream which he has interpreted as bad luck.

3. Benvolio is good humoured. He looks forward to the dance and he encourages the others not to waste time.

DRAMATIC EFFECT

1. This scene prepares the audience for the masque and builds up suspense. The audience know that Juliet will be there and that all Montagues are unwelcome.

2. The scene also reintroduces the notion of Fate. The audience fear for Romeo because of the dream he had and this also creates suspense.

3. The Queen Mab speech is a tour-de-force in terms of tone and mood. It is rich in imagery and it is said in a rush, as Mercutio's mind races with images of the fairy putting dreams in people's minds.

4. The scene also has great colour and movement. It is a street scene, with torch bearers and characters dressed for a party.

LANGUAGE

1. The language of Mercutio is witty and is filled with puns (see lines 40–41). His Queen Mab speech cleverly develops on an association of ideas with one image giving rise to another. It is a speech about the world of dream and nightmare. Although the content of his speech has to do with a dream world, the images themselves are sensual and the language is concrete.

2. Romeo's speech also makes use of puns (see lines 14–15). However, his language lacks the energy and playfulness of Mercutio's and tends to be more direct because he is still melancholic.

[SCENE V]

Introduction

This scene takes place in the Capulet household. It is filled with contrasts — youth and age, love and hate, movement and stillness. Romeo and Juliet meet for the first time and immediately fall in love. Their meeting is shadowed by the figure of Tybalt. He recognises Romeo and is intent on challenging him to a duel.

They march about the stage and Servingmen *come forth with napkins.*

First Ser. Where's Potpan that he helps not to take away?
He shift a trencher! He scrape a trencher!

Second Ser. When good manners shall lie all in one or two
men's hands, and they unwashed too, 'tis a foul
thing.   5

First Ser. Away with the joint-stools, remove the court-
cupboard, look to the plate. Good thou, save me a
piece of marchpane, and as thou loves me, let the
porter let in Susan Grindstone and Nell — Anthony,
and Potpan!   10

Third Ser. Ay boy, ready.

First Ser. You are looked for and called for, asked for and
sought for, in the great chamber.

Fourth Ser. We cannot be here and there too. Cheerly,
boys! Be brisk awhile, and the longer liver take all.   15

[Exeunt [Servingmen].

*Enter [*CAPULET, LADY CAPULET, JULIET, TYBALT, NURSE
and] all the Guests *and* Gentlewomen *to the Masquers.*

Cap.   Welcome, gentlemen, ladies that have their toes
Unplagu'd with corns will walk a bout with you.
Ah my mistresses, which of you all
Will now deny to dance? She that makes dainty,

Marginal glosses:

2 *trencher*
wood plate

8 *marchpane*
almond paste

17 *walk a bout*
dance
19 *makes dainty*
is shy

29

She I'll swear hath corns. Am I come near ye now?   20
Welcome, gentlemen. I have seen the day
That I have worn a visor and could tell
A whispering tale in a fair lady's ear,
Such as would please. 'Tis gone, 'tis gone, 'tis gone,
You are welcome, gentlemen: come, musicians, play.   25
A hall, a hall, give room! And foot it girls!

Music plays and they dance.

More light, you knaves, and turn the tables up.
And quench the fire, the room is grown too hot.
Ah sirrah, this unlook'd-for sport comes well.
Nay sit, nay sit, good cousin Capulet,   30
For you and I are past our dancing days.
How long is't now since last yourself and I
Were in a masque?

33 in a masque
in a dance

Capulet.   *You are welcome, gentlemen: come, musicians, play.*
        A hall, a hall, give room! And foot it girls!   lines 25–6

Cousin Cap.   By'r Lady, thirty years.
Cap.   What, man, 'tis not so much, 'tis not so much.
       'Tis since the nuptial of Lucentio,   35
       Come Pentecost as quickly as it will,
       Some five and twenty years: and then we masqu'd.
Cousin Cap. 'Tis more, 'tis more, his son is elder, sir:
       His son is thirty.

Cap.	Will you tell me that?	
	His son was but a ward two years ago.	40
Romeo.	What lady's that which doth enrich the hand	
	Of yonder knight?	
Ser.	I know not, sir.	
Romeo.	O, she doth teach the torches to burn bright.	
	It seems she hangs upon the cheek of night	
	As a rich jewel in an Ethiop's ear —	45
	Beauty too rich for use, for earth too dear.	
	So shows a snowy dove trooping with crows	
	As yonder lady o'er her fellows shows.	
	The measure done, I'll watch her place of stand,	
	And touching hers, make blessed my rude hand.	50
	Did my heart love till now? Forswear it, sight.	
	For I ne'er saw true beauty till this night.	
Tyb.	This by his voice should be a Montague.	
	Fetch me my rapier, boy. [*Exit Boy.*] What, dares the slave	
	Come hither, cover'd with an antic face,	55
	To fleer and scorn at our solemnity?	
	Now by the stock and honour of my kin,	
	To strike him dead I hold it not a sin.	
Cap.	Why how now, kinsman, wherefore storm you so?	
Tyb.	Uncle, this is a Montague, our foe:	60
	A villain that is hither come in spite	
	To scorn at our solemnity this night.	
Cap.	Young Romeo is it?	
Tyb.	'Tis he, that villain Romeo.	
Cap.	Content thee, gentle coz, let him alone,	
	A bears him like a portly gentleman;	65
	And, to say truth, Verona brags of him	
	To be a virtuous and well-govern'd youth.	
	I would not for the wealth of all this town	
	Here in my house do him disparagement.	
	Therefore be patient, take no note of him.	70
	It is my will, the which if thou respect,	

55 antic face
grotesque mask
56 fleer
to mock

69 disparagement
insult

	Show a fair presence and put off these frowns,	
	An ill-beseeming semblance for a feast.	
Tyb.	It fits when such a villain is a guest:	
	I'll not endure him.	

73 semblance expression

Cap.	He shall be endur'd.	75
	What, goodman boy! I say he shall! Go to,	
	Am I the master here or you? Go to,	
	You'll not endure him! God shall mend my soul,	
	You'll make a mutiny among my guests,	
	You will set cock-a-hoop, you'll be the man!	80
Tyb.	Why, uncle, 'tis a shame.	
Cap.	Go to, go to.	

80 set cock-a-hoop cause disorder

	You are a saucy boy. Is't so indeed?	
	This trick may chance to scathe you. I know what.	
	You must contrary me. Marry, 'tis time —	
	Well said, my hearts — You are a princox, go	85
	Be quiet, or — More light! More light! — For shame,	
	I'll make you quiet. What, cheerly, my hearts!	

85 princox upstart

Tyb.	Patience perforce with wilful choler meeting	
	Makes my flesh tremble in their different greeting.	
	I will withdraw; but this intrusion shall	90
	Now seeming sweet, convert to bitt'rest gall.	*Exit.*

88 Patience perforce with wilful choler meeting Patience meeting with anger

Romeo.	If I profane with my unworthiest hand	
	This holy shrine, the gentle sin is this:	
	My lips, two blushing pilgrims, ready stand	
	To smooth that rough touch with a tender kiss.	95

93 holy shrine Juliet

Juliet.	Good pilgrim, you do wrong your hand too much,	
	Which mannerly devotion shows in this;	
	For saints have hands that pilgrims' hands do touch,	
	And palm to palm is holy palmers' kiss.	

Romeo.	Have not saints lips, and holy palmers too?	100
Juliet.	Ay, pilgrim, lips that they must use in prayer.	
Romeo.	O then, dear saint, let lips do what hands do:	
	They pray: grant thou, lest faith turn to despair.	
Juliet.	Saints do not move, though grant for prayer's sake.	
Romeo.	Then move not, while my prayer's effect I take	105

99 holy palmers pilgrims

[*He kisses her.*]

Thus from my lips, by thine, my sin is purg'd.

Juliet. Then have my lips the sin that they have took.

Romeo. Sin from my lips? O trespass sweetly urg'd.

Give me my sin again.   [*He kisses her.*]

Juliet.   You kiss by th'book.

Nurse. Madam, your mother craves a word with you.   110

Romeo. What is her mother?

Nurse.   Marry bachelor

Her mother is the lady of the house,

And a good lady, and a wise and virtuous.

I nurs'd her daughter that you talk'd withal.

I tell you, he that can lay hold of her   115

Shall have the chinks.

109 *kiss by th' book* kiss conventionally, almost mechanically

116 *the chinks* riches, money

Romeo. *Sin from my lips? O trespass sweetly urg'd. Give me my sin again.*   *lines 108–9*

Romeo.   Is she a Capulet?

O dear account. My life is my foe's debt.

Ben. Away, be gone, the sport is at the best.

Romeo. Ay, so I fear; the more is my unrest.

Cap.	Nay, gentlemen, prepare not to be gone,	120
	We have a trifling foolish banquet towards.	

They whisper in his ear.

121 *towards*
coming, at hand

Is it e'en so? Why then, I thank you all;

I thank you honest gentlemen, good night.

More torches here. Come on then, let's to bed.

Ah sirrah, by my fay, it waxes late   125

I'll to my rest.

125 *waxes late*
getting late

[*Exeunt Capulet, Lady Capulet, Guests, Gentlewomen and Masquers.*]

Juliet.	Come hither Nurse. What is yond gentleman?
Nurse.	The son and heir of old Tiberio.
Juliet.	What's he that now is going out of door?
Nurse.	Marry, that I think be young Petruchio. 130
Juliet.	What's he that follows here, that would not dance?
Nurse.	I know not.
Juliet.	Go ask his name. If he be married,
	My grave is like to be my wedding bed.
Nurse.	His name is Romeo, and a Montague, 135
	The only son of your great enemy.
Juliet.	My only love sprung from my only hate.
	Too early seen unknown, and known too late.
	Prodigious birth of love it is to me
	That I must love a loathed enemy. 140
Nurse.	What's this? What's this?
Juliet.	A rhyme I learn'd even now
	Of one I danc'd withal. *One calls within: 'Juliet'.*
Nurse.	Anon, anon!
	Come let's away, the strangers all are gone. *Exeunt.*

139 *Prodigious*
Ill-fated

SCENE ANALYSIS

ACTION

1. Capulet greets his guests and encourages them to dance.

2. He discusses with his cousin how long it has been since either of them danced (more than twenty-five years).
3. Romeo sees Juliet and is stunned by her beauty.
4. Tybalt recognises Romeo by his voice and tells a servant to fetch his rapier, intending to kill Romeo.
5. Tybalt informs Capulet of Romeo's presence. Capulet advises Tybalt not to cause trouble.
6. Tybalt, in a temper at being forced to tolerate Romeo, leaves the feast with the intention of getting vengeance.
7. Romeo speaks to Juliet and kisses her.
8. Romeo learns from the Nurse that Juliet is Capulet's daughter.
9. Juliet learns from the Nurse that Romeo is the son of her father's enemy.

THEMES

1. Again, the themes of the feud and hatred are to the fore in Tybalt's tantrum and his eagerness to fight Romeo.
2. The first meeting of Romeo and Juliet presents the theme of love.
3. Time as an agent in all human affairs is introduced in the conversation between the Capulet cousins.

CHARACTERISATION

1. Tybalt again emerges as a person who causes tension and conflict. He appears as petulant and dangerous.
2. Capulet seems almost reasonable and is a good host.
3. Juliet is an intelligent young woman who is beautiful, witty and charming. Her exchange of remarks with Romeo shows that she is his equal and her own willingness to be kissed and to kiss reveals her to be as passionate as he is.
4. Romeo is portrayed as a sophisticated young man who is confident and charming. His wooing of Juliet is conventional — as suggested by the use of their sonnet — but he is sincere in his loveplaying.

DRAMATIC EFFECT

1. The scene provides a wonderful contrast between age and youth, and between hatred and love.
2. There is great tension and suspense in the scene: the lovers' first meeting, the threat of Tybalt.
3. There is wonderful colour and movement in the scene: the guests dance and are in costumes for a masked ball.

4. The scene has both humour (the exchanges of the lovers) and passion (Tybalt's fury), so it provides tension and light relief.

5. The scene has a fast rhythm with a lot of action, and contains elements of climax and anti-climax.

LANGUAGE

1. The exchange between Tybalt and Capulet is in prose. The language is realistic, as is the conversation between Capulet and his cousin.

2. The lovers' exchange takes the form of a sonnet until they first kiss. Romeo uses the sustained metaphor of a pilgrim visiting a shrine and Juliet takes up his lead as they play a poetic game that is a wooing.

[ACT II]
[PROLOGUE]

[Enter] CHORUS

Chorus.   Now old desire doth in his deathbed lie

And young affection gapes to be his heir;

That fair for which love groan'd for and would die,

With tender Juliet match'd, is now not fair.

Now Romeo is belov'd and loves again,   5

Alike bewitched by the charm of looks,

But to his foe suppos'd he must complain

And she steal love's sweet bait from fearful hooks.

Being held a foe, he may not have access

To breathe such vows as lovers use to swear;   10

And she as much in love, her means much less

To meet her new beloved anywhere.

But passion lends them power, time means, to meet,

Tempering extremities with extreme sweet.   [Exit.]

[SCENE I]

Introduction

Romeo separates from his companions, intent on going back to see Juliet. Mercutio jokes about love being nothing more than lust.

Enter ROMEO *alone.*

Romeo.	Can I go forward when my heart is here?
	Turn back, dull earth, and find thy centre out.

[Withdraws.]

Enter BENVOLIO *with* MERCUTIO.

Ben.	Romeo! My cousin Romeo! Romeo!
Mer.	He is wise,
	And on my life hath stol'n him home to bed.
Ben.	He ran this way and leapt this orchard wall. 5
	Call, good Mercutio.
Mer.	Nay, I'll conjure too:
	Romeo! Humours! Madman! Passion! Lover!
	Appear thou in the likeness of a sigh,
	Speak but one rhyme and I am satisfied.
	Cry but 'Ay me!' Pronounce but 'love' and 'dove', 10
	Speak to my gossip Venus one fair word,
	One nickname for her purblind son and heir,
	Young Abraham Cupid, he that shot so trim
	When King Cophetua lov'd the beggar maid.
	He heareth not, he stirreth not, he moveth not: 15
	The ape is dead and I must conjure him.
	I conjure thee by Rosaline's bright eyes,
	By her high forehead and her scarlet lip,
	By her fine foot, straight leg, and quivering thigh,
	And the demesnes that there adjacent lie, 20
	That in thy likeness thou appear to us.
Ben.	And if he hear thee, thou wilt anger him.

2 *dull earth*
dull rascal

11 *gossip*
friend
12 *purblind*
completely blind
13 *Abraham
Cupid*
character in
popular ballad

20 *demesnes*
places, domains

Mer.	This cannot anger him. 'Twould anger him
	To raise a spirit in his mistress' circle
	Of some strange nature, letting it there stand 25
	Till she had laid it and conjur'd it down:
	That were some spite. My invocation
	Is fair and honest; in his mistress' name
	I conjure only but to raise up him.
Ben.	Come, he hath hid himself among these trees 30
	To be consorted with the humorous night.
	Blind is his love, and best befits the dark.
Mer.	If love be blind, love cannot hit the mark.
	Now will he sit under a medlar tree
	And wish his mistress were that kind of fruit 35
	As maids call medlars when they laugh alone.
	O Romeo, that she were, O that she were
	An open-arse and thou a poperin pear!
	Romeo, good night. I'll to my truckle-bed.
	This field-bed is too cold for me to sleep. 40
	Come, shall we go?
Ben.	Go then, for 'tis in vain
	To seek him here that means not to be found.

27 invocation
calling

31 To be consorted with the humorous night.
To be close to the damp night.

39 truckle-bed
small bed on wheels
40 field-bed
camp bed

Exeunt [Benvolio and Mercutio]

SCENE ANALYSIS

ACTION

1. Romeo slips away from his friends, determined to meet Juliet again.
2. Mercutio and Benvolio jest about where he might be and Mercutio jokingly tries to conjure up his friend with reference to Rosaline and vulgar remarks about love.

THEMES

The major theme here is that of love. Romeo is now enchanted by Juliet and cannot leave the Capulet house. In contrast with his love, there is Mercutio's mockery of love. Mercutio views love in physical and sexual terms. His ridiculing of Rosaline reveals how Romeo's love for her was no more than a 'crush'.

CHARACTERISATION

1. Mercutio emerges as a very witty and irreverent individual. His mockery of Romeo's lovesick mood is wonderfully tasteless and satirical, showing his contempt for sentiment.
2. Benvolio once again appears as a voice of reason. He tries to get Mercutio to be less cutting in his jibes, saying 'thou wilt anger him'. However, his reasoning is to no avail. He suggests that they leave Romeo to his quest for love.

DRAMATIC EFFECT

1. This is a transition scene acting as a link between the crowded setting of the Capulet feast and the intimacy of the balcony scene which follows it. It contains great humour, dominated by the wit of Mercutio.
2. The scene also suggests how the love of the two teenagers will distance them from those around them; so it has a symbolic function.

LANGUAGE

Mercutio's language is crude in its imagery. His speeches are filled with sexual connotations which reduce love to mere lust.

[SCENE II]

Introduction

Romeo enters the Capulet gardens and is beneath Juliet's balcony. She professes her love for him. He then swears his love for her. She constantly looks for him to express himself sincerely and to commit himself to her. They exchange vows and she says she will send a messenger the following day to find out what time they will marry.

[*Romeo comes forward.*]

Romeo.   He jests at scars that never felt a wound.

[*Enter* JULIET *above.*]

But soft, what light through yonder window breaks?
It is the east and Juliet is the sun!
Arise fair sun and kill the envious moon
Who is already sick and pale with grief   5
That thou her maid art far more fair than she.
Be not her maid since she is envious,
Her vestal livery is but sick and green   8 *vestal livery*
And none but fools do wear it. Cast it off.   virgin uniform
It is my lady, O it is my love!   10
O that she knew she were!
She speaks, yet she says nothing. What of that?
Her eye discourses, I will answer it.   13 *discourses*
I am too bold. 'Tis not to me she speaks.   speaks love's
Two of the fairest stars in all the heaven,   15   language
Having some business, do entreat her eyes
To twinkle in their spheres till they return.
What if her eyes were there, they in her head?
The brightness of her cheek would shame those stars
As daylight doth a lamp. Her eyes in heaven   20

Would through the airy region stream so bright

That birds would sing and think it were not night.

See how she leans her cheek upon her hand.

O that I were a glove upon that hand,

That I might touch that cheek.

Juliet.   Ay me.

Romeo.   She speaks.   25

O speak again bright angel, for thou art

As glorious to this night, being o'er my head,

As is a winged messenger of heaven

Unto the white-upturned wondering eyes

Of mortals that fall back to gaze on him   30

When he bestrides the lazy-puffing clouds

And sails upon the bosom of the air.

Juliet.   O Romeo, Romeo, wherefore art thou Romeo?

learn Deny thy father and refuse thy name.

this   Or if thou wilt not, be but sworn my love   35

N.B!   And I'll no longer be a Capulet

Romeo.   Shall I hear more, or shall I speak at this?

Juliet.   'Tis but thy name that is my enemy:

Thou art thyself, though not a Montague.

What's Montague? It is nor hand nor foot   40

Nor arm nor face nor any other part

Belonging to a man. O be some other name.

What's in a name? That which we call a rose

By any other word would smell as sweet;

So Romeo would, were he not Romeo call'd,   45

Retain that dear perfection which he owes

Without that title. Romeo, doff thy name,

And for thy name, which is no part of thee,

Take all myself.

Romeo. *speaks*   I take thee at thy word.

Call me but love and I'll be new baptis'd: 50

Henceforth I never will be Romeo.

Juliet.   What man art thou that thus bescreen'd in night

So stumblest on my counsel?

46 *owes*
possesses
47 *doff*
give up

53 *stumblest on
my counsel*
overhear my
thoughts

Romeo.   By a name
        I know not how to tell thee who I am:
        My name, dear saint, is hateful to myself   55
        Because it is an enemy to thee.
        Had I it written, I would tear the word.

Juliet.   My ears have yet not drunk a hundred words
        Of thy tongue's uttering, yet I know the sound.
        Art thou not Romeo, and a Montague?   60
        Romeo Neither, fair maid, if either thee dislike.

Juliet.   How cam'st thou hither, tell me, and wherefore?
        The orchard walls are high and hard to climb,
        And the place death, considering who thou art,
        If any of my kinsmen find thee here.   65

Romeo.   With love's light wings did I o'erperch these walls,
        for stony limits cannot hold love out,
        And what love can do, that dares love attempt:
        Therefore thy kinsmen are no stop to me.

Juliet.   If they do see thee, they will murder thee.   70

Romeo.   Alack, there lies more peril in thine eye
        Than twenty of their swords. Look thou but sweet
        And I am proof against their enmity.

Juliet.   I would not for the world they saw thee here.

Romeo.   I have night's cloak to hide me from their eyes,   75
        And but thou love me, let them find me here.
        My life were better ended by their hate
        Than death prorogued, wanting of thy love.

Juliet.   By whose direction found'st thou out this place?

Romeo.   By love, that first did prompt me to enquire.   80
        He lent me counsel, and I lent him eyes.
        I am no pilot, yet wert thou as far
        As that vast shore wash'd with the farthest sea,
        I should adventure for such merchandise.

Juliet.   Thou knowest the mask of night is on my face,   85
        Else would a maiden blush bepaint my cheek
        For that which thou hast heard me speak tonight.
        Fain would I dwell on form; fain, fain deny

66 o'erperch
fly over
67 stony limits
boundary walls

78 prorogued
postponed

88 Fain
Gladly
dwell on form
do the correct
thing

handwritten notes: "very dramatic", "he would sail to the end of the world for Julie"

43

Juliet.   *Dost thou love me? I know thou wilt say 'Ay',*
           And I will take thy word.   *lines 90–91*

What I have spoke. But farewell, compliment.

Dost thou love me? I know thou wilt say 'Ay',   90

And I will take thy word. Yet, if thou swear'st,

Thou mayst prove false. At lovers' perjuries,

They say, Jove laughs. O gentle Romeo,

If thou dost love, pronounce it faithfully.

Or, if thou think'st I am too quickly won,   95

very metuir + sensable

89 *compliment*
convention,
proper behaviour

93 *Jove*
King of Roman
fools

44

I'll frown and be perverse and say thee nay,

So thou wilt woo; but else, not for the world.

In truth, fair Montague, I am too fond,

And therefore thou mayst think my haviour light,

But trust me, gentleman, I'll prove more true   100

Than those that have more cunning to be strange.

I should have been more strange, I must confess,

But that thou overheard'st, ere I was ware,

My true-love passion; therefore pardon me,

And not impute this yielding to light love   105

Which the dark night hath so discovered.

Romeo.   Lady, by yonder blessed moon I vow,

That tips with silver all these fruit-tree tops —

Juliet.   O swear not by the moon, th'inconstant moon,

That monthly changes in her circled orb,   110

Lest that thy love prove likewise variable.

Romeo.   What shall I swear by?

Juliet.   Do not swear at all.

Or if thou wilt, swear by thy gracious self,

Which is the god of my idolatry,

And I'll believe thee.

Romeo.   If my heart's dear love —   115

Juliet.   Well, do not swear. Although I joy in thee,

I have no joy of this contract tonight:

It is too rash, too unadvis'd, too sudden,

Too like the lightning, which doth cease to be

Ere one can say 'It lightens'. Sweet, good night.   120

This bud of love, by summer's ripening breath,

May prove a beauteous flower when next we meet.

Good night, good night. As sweet repose and rest

Come to thy heart as that within my breast.

Romeo.   O wilt thou leave me so unsatisfied?   125

Juliet.   What satisfaction canst thou have tonight?

Romeo.   Th'exchange of thy love's faithful vow for mine.

Juliet.   I gave thee mine before thou didst request it,

And yet I would it were to give again.

101 *strange*
reserved

109 *inconstant*
changeable

Romeo.	Wouldst thou withdraw it? For what purpose, love?	130
Juliet.	But to be frank and give it thee again;	
	And yet I wish but for the thing I have.	
	My bounty is as boundless as the sea,	
	My love as deep; the more I give to thee	
	The more I have, for both are infinite	135
	I hear some noise within. Dear love, adieu.	

133 bounty
generosity, gifts

[*Nurse calls within.*]

Anon, good Nurse — Sweet Montague be true.

Stay but a little, I will come again.   [*Exit Juliet.*]

Romeo.   O blessed blessed night. I am afeard,

Being in night, all this is but a dream,   140

Too flattering sweet to be substantial.

[*Enter JULIET above.*]

141 substantial
real

Juliet.   Three words, dear Romeo, and good night indeed.

If that thy bent of love be honourable,

Thy purpose marriage, send me word tomorrow

By one that I'll procure to come to thee,   145

Where and what time thou wilt perform the rite,

And all my fortunes at thy foot I'll lay,

145 procure
arrange

And follow thee my lord throughout the world.

Nurse.   [*Within.*] Madam.

Juliet.   I come, anon — But if thou meanest not well   150

I do beseech thee —

Nurse.   [*Within.*]   Madam.

Juliet.   By and by I come —

To cease thy strife and leave me to my grief.

Tomorrow will I send.

Romeo.   So thrive my soul —

Juliet.   A thousand times good night   [*Exit Juliet.*]

Romeo.   A thousand times the worse, to want thy light.   155

Love goes toward love as schoolboys from their books,

But love from love, toward school with heavy looks.

Enter JULIET [*above*] *again.*

Juliet.	Hist! Romeo, hist! O for a falconer's voice
	To lure this tassel-gentle back again.
	Bondage is hoarse and may not speak aloud, 160
	Else would I tear the cave where Echo lies
	And make her airy tongue more hoarse than mine
	With repetition of my Romeo's name.
Romeo.	It is my soul that calls upon my name.
	How silver-sweet sound lovers' tongues by night, 165
	Like softest music to attending ears.
Juliet.	Romeo.
Romeo.	My nyas.
Juliet.	What o'clock tomorrow
	Shall I send to thee?
Romeo.	By the hour of nine.
Juliet.	I will not fail. 'Tis twenty year till then.
	I have forgot why I did call thee back. 170
Romeo.	Let me stand here till thou remember it.
Juliet.	I shall forget, to have thee still stand there,
	Remembering how I love thy company.
Romeo.	And I'll still stay to have thee still forget,
	Forgetting any other home but this. 175
Juliet.	'Tis almost morning, I would have thee gone,
	And yet no farther than a wanton's bird,
	That lets it hop a little from his hand
	Like a poor prisoner in his twisted gyves,
	And with a silken thread plucks it back again, 180
	So loving-jealous of his liberty.
Romeo.	I would I were thy bird.
Juliet.	Sweet, so would I:
	Yet I should kill thee with much cherishing.
	Good night, good night. Parting is such sweet sorrow
	That I shall say good night till it be morrow. 185

[*Exit Juliet.*]

158 *Hist*
Listen
159 *tassel-gentle*
male falcon
160 *Bondage is
hoarse*
Under my father's
control I must
whisper
161 *Echo*
a nymph who,
when rejected,
dwells as a voice in
caves
167 *My nyas*
My dear (falcon
term)

177 *wanton's bird*
an irresponsible
girl's pet
179 *gyves*
straps, chains,
fetters

Romeo.	Sleep dwell upon thine eyes, peace in thy breast.	
	Would I were sleep and peace so sweet to rest.	
	The grey-ey'd morn smiles on the frowning night,	
	Chequering the eastern clouds with streaks of light;	192 *ghostly Sire*
	And darkness fleckled like a drunkard reels 190	spiritual father, priest
	From forth day's pathway, made by Titan's wheels.	193 *dear hap*
	Hence will I to my ghostly Sire's close cell,	good luck or
	His help to crave and my dear hap to tell. *Exit.*	fortune

SCENE ANALYSIS

ACTION

1. Romeo enters the Capulet grounds and sees Juliet come to the balcony outside her bedroom.
2. Juliet declares her love for Romeo, not knowing that he is listening. She says that it is only his name that is her enemy and that he should surrender it.
3. Romeo makes his presence known and says that he will no longer be named Montague.
4. Juliet fears for his safety and urges him to leave, but he says that night will protect him.
5. She claims that he should not have heard what she said, that she should have been more reserved, but that her love is sincere.
6. He declares his own love for her, although she urges him not to use conventional expression, but to speak it sincerely.
7. Juliet says that if his intentions are marriage, he should arrange their wedding for the following day. She will send a messenger to get the information from him.

CHARACTERISATION

1. Romeo is now more decisive than ever. He has risked being found by his enemies to see Juliet again: 'Thy kinsmen are no stop to me'. His melancholy appears to have gone and he is completely committed to winning Juliet:

> I am no pilot, yet wert thou as far
> As that vast shore wash'd with the farthest sea,
> I should adventure for such merchandise.

He is initially confused by her instructions that he should not express himself in the clichéd language of love: 'What shall I swear by?', but he is obviously sincere, willing to sacrifice his name: 'My name, dear saint, is hateful to myself' and has no fear of dangers when the prize is Juliet:

> My life were better ended by their hate [the Capulets]
> Than death prorogued, wanting of thy love.

Obviously then, the scene indicates the effect that Juliet has had on Romeo.

2. Juliet tends to be the more mature and sensible of the lovers. At the Capulet feast, she gently teased him about kissing 'by the book'. Now she corrects him in his efforts to declare his love for her:

> O swear not by the moon, th' inconstant moon,
> That monthly changes in her circled orb
> Lest that thy love prove likewise variable.

She is very much in love and although she is embarrassed at having been overheard, she decides to make her love clear:

> . . . I'll prove more true
> Than those that have more cunning to be strange.

She is aware of the dangers that they face and warns Romeo to be careful: 'If they do see thee they will kill thee'. In other words, her love is tempered by a practical outlook. She is concerned by the suddenness of their relationship:

> I have no joy of this contract tonight:
> It is too rash, too unadvis'd, too sudden.

Yet she discovers that love overwhelms her, she recognises that her heart belongs to Romeo. She takes the initiative and tells Romeo that if he is really sincere, then he should arrange their marriage and send for her:

> If that thy bent of love be honourable,
> Thy purpose marriage, send me word to-morrow.

These lines reveal that although Juliet is in love, it is a love directed by a measure of sense. In this scene, she reveals herself to be independent — knowing her mind and acting upon her feelings — and decisive.

THEMES

The main theme of this scene is that of love. The two young lovers declare their commitment to each other and exchange vows. They attempt to deny the world of the feud. They wish to ignore their names and their identities. Yet, Juliet is aware that if Romeo is caught in the garden he will be killed, so the love of the couple is shadowed by the presence of the feud.

DRAMATIC EFFECT

1. Coming after the Capulet feast, this scene is very intimate. The setting is romantic (night, a garden and a balcony) and picturesque, and the topic of conversation is the feelings of the lovers for each other.
2. The depth of their love for each other is made evident in their willingness to sacrifice everything.
3. The scene has some suspense: Romeo could be discovered by Juliet's kinsmen; Juliet is called indoors and he risks discovery outside; he may fail to express his love in a manner that pleases her. Also, the scene gradually moves towards a climax, when Juliet asks him if his intention is marriage. All of these aspects engage the audience.

LANGUAGE

The language of the scene is wonderful in its imagery and energy. The lovers use figurative speech, filled with metaphor and simile, to express their feelings for each other:

> My bounty is as boundless as the sea,
> My love as deep: the more I give to thee,
> The more I have, for both are infinite. (Juliet)

> It is the east and Juliet is the sun!
> Arise fair sun and kill the envious moon . . . (Romeo)

> O for a falconer's voice
> To lure this tassle-gentle back again. (Juliet)

It is also a language filled with hyperbole (exaggeration) which mirrors the lovers' devotion to each other:

A thousand times good-night! (Juliet)

Yet I should kill thee with much cherishing. (Juliet)

The brightness of her cheek would shame those stars
As daylight doth a lamp. (Romeo)

Essentially, the lovers try, through metaphor, to create an alternative world to that of
the feud, thus attempting to ignore the real world. It is an important scene because it
is the moment when the lovers withdraw from the feud into a parallel, private world of
night and dreams.

[SCENE III]

Introduction

*Romeo goes to Friar Lawrence to arrange his marriage with Juliet. The Friar
worries that Romeo is insincere but sees an opportunity to unite the feuding
households and agrees to marry the lovers that day.*

Enter FRIAR [LAURENCE] *alone with a basket.*

Friar L.	Now, ere the sun advance his burning eye
	The day to cheer, and night's dank dew to dry,
	I must upfill the osier cage of ours
	With baleful weeds and precious-juiced flowers.
	The earth that's nature's mother is her tomb:

3 osier cage
willow basket

4 baleful
harmful,
poisonous

The earth that's nature's mother is her tomb: 5
What is her burying grave, that is her womb;
And from her womb children of divers kind
We sucking on her natural bosom find.
Many for many virtues excellent,
None but for some, and yet all different.   10
O, mickle is the powerful grace that lies

11 mickle
great

In plants, herbs, stones, and their true qualities.
For naught so vile that on the earth doth live
But to the earth some special good doth give;
Nor aught so good but, strain'd from that fair use,   15
Revolts from true birth, stumbling on abuse.
Virtue itself turns vice being misapplied,
And vice sometime's by action dignified.

Enter ROMEO

Within the infant rind of this weak flower
Poison hath residence, and medicine power: 20
For this, being smelt, with that part cheers each part;
Being tasted, stays all senses with the heart.
Two such opposed kings encamp them still
In man as well as herbs: grace and rude will;
And where the worser is predominant   25
Full soon the canker death eats up that plant.

Romeo. Good morrow, father.
Friar L.   Benedicte.
What early tongue so sweet saluteth me?
Young son, it argues a distemper'd head
So soon to bid good morrow to thy bed.   30
Care keeps his watch in every old man's eye,
And where care lodges sleep will never lie,
But where unbruised youth with unstuff'd brain
Doth couch his limbs, there golden sleep doth reign.
Therefore thy earliness doth me assure   35
Thou art uprous'd with some distemperature;
Or, if not so, then here I hit it right:
Our Romeo hath not been in bed tonight.
Romeo. That last is true. The sweeter rest was mine.
Friar L. God pardon sin. Was thou with Rosaline?   40
Romeo. With Rosaline! My ghostly father, no.
I have forgot that name, and that name's woe.
Friar L. That's my good son. But where hast thou been then?

15 *strain'd*	turned away
18 *by action dignified*	by the was it is used it becomes dignified
19 *infant rind*	seedling's talk
21 *that part*	that quality, its scent
26 *canker*	destructive
28 *Benedicte*	Bless you
29 *distemper'd head*	troubled mind
33 *unstuff'd brain*	untroubled

Romeo.	I'll tell thee ere thou ask it me again.	
	I have been feasting with mine enemy,	45
	Where on a sudden one hath wounded me	
	That's by me wounded. Both our remedies	
	Within thy help and hold physic lies.	
	I bear no hatred, blessed man, for lo,	
	My intercession likewise steads my foe.	50
Friar L.	Be plain, good son, and homely in thy drift;	
	Riddling confession finds but riddling shrift.	
Romeo.	Then plainly know my heart's dear love is set	
	On the fair daughter of rich Capulet.	

48 physic
healing power
50 intercession
appeal
steads my foe
benefits my enemy
51 homely
plain
52 riddling shrift
doubtful pardon

Romeo.   *Then plainly know my heart's dear love is set*
         On the fair daughter of rich Capulet.   lines 53–4

	As mine on hers, so hers is set on mine,	55
	And all combin'd save what thou must combine	
	By holy marriage. When, and where, and how	
	We met, we woo'd, and made exchange of vow	
	I'll tell thee as we pass; but this I pray,	
	That thou consent to marry us today.	60
Friar L.	Holy Saint Francis! What a change is here!	
	Is Rosaline, that thou didst love so dear,	
	So soon forsaken? Young men's love then lies	
	Not truly in their hearts but in their eyes.	
	Jesu Maria! What a deal of brine	65

Hath wash'd thy sallow cheeks for Rosaline.

How much salt water thrown away in waste

To season love, that of it doth not taste.

The sun not yet thy sighs from heaven clears,

Thy old groans yet ring in mine ancient ears.   70

Lo here upon thy cheek the stain doth sit

Of an old tear that is not wash'd off yet.

If ere thou wast thyself, and these woes thine,

Thou and these woes were all for Rosaline.

And art thou chang'd? Pronounce this sentence then:

Women may fall when there's no strength in men.   76

Romeo.   Thou chid'st me oft for loving Rosaline.

Friar L.   For doting, not for loving, pupil mine.

Romeo.   And bad'st me bury love.

Friar L.   Not in a grave

To lay one in, another out to have.   80

Romeo.   I pray thee chide me not, her I love now

Doth grace for grace and love for love allow.

The other did not so.

Friar L.   O, she knew well

Thy love did read by rote that could not spell.

But come young waverer, come, go with me,   85

In one respect I'll thy assistant be.

For this alliance may so happy prove

To turn your households' rancour to pure love.

Romeo.   O let us hence: I stand on sudden haste.

Friar L.   Wisely and slow; they stumble that run fast.   90

Exeunt.

68 *To season love*
To preserve love

84 *Thy love did read*
by rote that could
not spell.
Your love was that
of a child who
recites without
understanding
88 *rancour*
hatred

54

SCENE ANALYSIS

ACTION

1. Friar Lawrence is about to search for medicinal herbs. He reflects on the good and evil that co-exist in herbs and how it is also the case with man.
2. Romeo enters and his early arrival makes the Friar fear that the young man spent the night with Rosaline.
3. Romeo tells the Friar of his love for Juliet and asks the priest to perform a wedding ceremony.
4. Friar Lawrence accuses Romeo of fickleness and insincerity. However, he sees the union of Romeo and Juliet as an opportunity to unite their families and agrees to the marriage.

THEMES

1. The scene begins with reflections on the nature of life, which contains both good and evil.
2. The theme of love is also discussed. Romeo's courtly love for Rosaline is contrasted with his romantic love for Juliet.

CHARACTERISATION

1. Romeo's sincerity is apparent in this scene. His commitment to Juliet is obvious:

   > Then plainly know my heart's dear love is set
   > On the fair daughter of rich Capulet.

   He is determined to be married to Juliet and will not be swayed by criticism: '. . . consent to marry us today . . . I stand on sudden haste'. This is a very changed Romeo to the moody and melodramatic figure who appeared in the opening scene.
2. Friar Lawrence is portrayed as a wise and knowledgeable man. He has an understanding of nature and of life:

   > For naught so vile that on the earth doth live
   > But to the earth some special good doth give.

   He recognises that life balances the good and the bad:

   > Two such opposed kings encamp them still
   > In man as well as herbs: grace and rude will;

And where the worser is predominant
Full soon the canker death eats up that plant.

He means well in agreeing to marry the lovers:

In one respect I'll thy assistant be.
For this alliance may so happy prove
To turn your households' rancour to pure love.

DRAMATIC EFFECT

1. In this scene the plot is moved forward with arrangements being made for the marriage.
2. It is a contemplative scene which encourages consideration of why there is wickedness in the world and how love has different aspects.
3. It contrasts the passion of youth with the sagacity of age.

LANGUAGE

1. The imagery of the scene initially focuses on herbs and their powers to harm or heal.
2. Friar Lawrence uses many metaphors and in contrasting the world of nature and that of man, he draws an analogy between them.
3. Romeo's language is colloquial, although his tone is emotive and passionate.

[SCENE IV]

Introduction

Benvolio and Mercutio fear that Romeo has been challenged to a duel by Tybalt and that Romeo will be no match for him. They meet Romeo and find him in good humour. The Nurse also looks for Romeo so that she can take his message to Juliet. He tells the Nurse to have Juliet meet him at Friar Lawrence's that afternoon to be married.

Enter BENVOLIO *and* MERCUTIO.

Mer.   Where the devil should this Romeo be? Came he
not home tonight?

Ben.	Not to his father's; I spoke with his man.
Mer.	Why, that same pale hard-hearted wench, that
	Rosaline, torments him so that he will sure run mad. 5
Ben.	Tybalt, the kinsman to old Capulet, hath sent a
	letter to his father's house.
Mer.	A challenge, on my life.
Ben.	Romeo will answer it.
Mer.	Any man that can write may answer a letter. 10
Ben.	Nay, he will answer the letter's master, how he
	dares, being dared.
Mer.	Alas poor Romeo, he is already dead, stabbed with
	a white wench's black eye, run through the ear with
	a love song, the very pin of his heart cleft with the 15
	blind bow-boy's butt-shaft. And is he a man to
	encounter Tybalt?
Ben.	Why, what is Tybalt?
Mer.	More than Prince of Cats. O, he's the courageous
	captain of compliments: he fights as you sing prick- 20
	song, keeps time, distance and proportion. He rests
	his minim rests, one, two, and the third in your
	bosom: the very butcher of a silk button — a
	duellist, a duellist, a gentleman of the very first
	house, of the first and second cause. Ah, the im- 25
	mortal passado, the punto reverso, the hay!
Ben.	The what?
Mer.	The pox of such antic lisping affecting phantasimes,
	these new tuners of accent. By Jesu, a very good
	blade, a very tall man, a very good whore! Why, is 30
	not this a lamentable thing, grandsire, that we
	should be thus afflicted with these strange flies,
	these fashion-mongers, these 'pardon-me's', who
	stand so much on the new form that they cannot
	sit at ease on the old bench? O their bones, their 35
	bones!

16 *bow-boy's butt-shaft*
Cupid's blunt arrow
20 *compliments*
formalities
prick-song
music noted down
22 *minim*
briefest
23 *butcher of a silk button*
good duellist
25-26 *immortal passado*
lunge
punto reverso
reverse strike
28 *phantasimes*
absurd persons

33 *'pardon-me's'*
fops

Enter ROMEO.

Ben.	Here comes Romeo, here comes Romeo!

Mer.	Without his roe, like a dried herring. O flesh, flesh, how art thou fishified. Now is he for the numbers that Petrarch flowed in. Laura, to his lady, was a kitchen wench — marry, she had a better love to berhyme her — Dido a dowdy, Cleopatra a gypsy, Helen and Hero hildings and harlots, Thisbe a grey eye or so, but not to the purpose. Signor Romeo, bonjour. There's a French salutation to your French slop. You gave us the counterfeit fairly last night.
Romeo.	Good morrow to you both. What counterfeit did I give you?
Mer.	The slip sir, the slip. Can you not conceive?
Romeo.	Pardon, good Mercutio, my business was great, and in such a case as mine a man may strain courtesy.
Mer.	That's as much as to say, such a case as yours constrains a man to bow in the hams.
Romeo.	Meaning to curtsy.
Mer.	Thou hast most kindly hit it.
Romeo.	A most courteous exposition.
Mer.	Nay, I am the very pink of courtesy.
Romeo.	Pink for flower.
Mer.	Right.
Romeo.	Why, then is my pump well flowered.
Mer.	Sure wit, follow me this jest now, till thou hast worn out thy pump, that when the single sole of it is worn, the jest may remain after the wearing solely singular.
Romeo.	O single-soled jest, solely singular for the singleness.
Mer.	Come between us, good Benvolio, my wits faints.
Romeo.	Switch and spurs, switch and spurs, or I'll cry a match!
Mer.	Nay, if our wits run the wild-goose chase I am done. For thou hast more of the wild-goose in one of thy

40

45

46 *slop*
baggy trousers

50

50 *conceive*
understand

55

55 *hams*
knees

60

62 *pump*
shoe

65

70

wits than I am sure I have in my whole five. Was I
with you there for the goose?   75

Romeo.   Thou wast never with me for anything, when
thou wast not there for the goose.

Mer.   I will bite thee by the ear for that jest.

Romeo.   Nay, good goose, bite not.

Mer.   Thy wit is a very bitter sweeting, it is a most sharp   80
sauce.

Romeo.   And is it not then well served in to a sweet goose?

Mer.   O here's a wit of cheveril, that stretches from an
inch narrow to an ell broad.

Romeo.   I stretch it out for that word 'broad', which,   85
added to the goose, proves thee far and wide a
broad goose.

Mer.   Why, is not this better now than groaning for
love? Now art thou sociable, now art thou Romeo;
now art thou what thou art, by art as well as by   90
nature. For this drivelling love is like a great natural
that runs lolling up and down to hide his bauble in
a hole.

Ben.   Stop there, stop there.

Mer.   Thou desirest me to stop in my tale against the hair.   95

Ben.   Thou wouldst else have made thy tale large.

Mer.   O thou art deceived; I would have made it short;
for I was come to the whole depth of my tale and
meant indeed to occupy the argument no longer.

Romeo.   Here's goodly gear.   100

Enter NURSE *and her* man [PETER].

A sail! A sail!

Mer.   Two. Two. A shirt and a smock.

Nurse.   Peter.

Peter.   Anon.

Nurse.   My fan, Peter.   105

Mer.   Good Peter, to hide her face, for her fan's the
fairer face.

83 cheveril
of good kid leather
84 ell
forty-five inches

91 great natural
fool, clown
92 bauble
stick
95 against the hair
(which goes)
against the grain
96 large
vulgar

100 goodly gear
Nurse looking like
a bundle of cloths

Nurse.   God ye good morrow, gentlemen.

Mer.   God ye good e'en, fair gentlewoman.

Nurse.   Is it good e'en?   110

Mer.   'Tis no less, I tell ye; for the bawdy hand of the
           dial is now upon the prick of noon.

Nurse.   Out upon you. What a man are you?

Romeo.   One, gentlewoman, that God hath made, him-
           self to mar.   115

Nurse.   By my troth it is well said; 'for himself to mar'
           quoth a? Gentlemen, can any of you tell me where
           I may find the young Romeo?

Romeo.   I can tell you; but young Romeo will be older
           when you have found him than he was when you   120
           sought him. I am the youngest of that name, for
           fault of a worse.

Nurse.   You say well.

Mer.   Yea, is the worst well? Very well took i'faith.
           Wisely, wisely.   125

Nurse.   If you be he sir, I desire some confidence with you.

Ben.   She will endite him to some supper.   *127 endite*
                                                                  write

Mer.   A bawd! A bawd! A Bawd! So ho.

Romeo.   What hast thou found?

Mer.   No hare, sir, unless a hare, sir, in a lenten pie, that   130
           is something stale and hoar ere it be spent.

                              He walks by them and sings.

               An old hare hoar,

               And an old hare hoar,

               Is very good meat in Lent.

                         But a hare that is hoar   135

               Is too much for a score

               When it hoars ere it be spent.

           Romeo, will you come to your father's? We'll to
           dinner thither.

Romeo.   I will follow you.   140

Mer.   Farewell, ancient lady, farewell, lady, lady, lady.

                              Exeunt Mercutio and Benvolio.

Nurse.	I pray you, sir, what saucy merchant was this, that was so full of his ropery?
Romeo.	A gentleman, Nurse, that loves to hear himself talk, and will speak more in a minute than he will 145 stand to in a month.
Nurse.	And a speak anything against me I'll take him down, and a were lustier than he is, and twenty such jacks. And if I cannot, I'll find those that shall. Scurvy knave! I am none of his flirt-gills, I am none 150 of his skains-mates. *She turns to Peter her man.* And thou must stand by too and suffer every knave to use me at his pleasure!
Peter.	I saw no man use you at his pleasure; if I had, my weapon should quickly have been out. I warrant 155 you, I dare draw as soon as another man, if I see occasion in a good quarrel, and the law on my side.
Nurse.	Now afore God I am so vexed that every part about me quivers. Scurvy knave. Pray you, sir, a word — and as I told you, my young lady bid me 160 enquire you out. What she bid me say, I will keep to myself. But first let me tell ye, if ye should lead her in a fool's paradise, as they say, it were a very gross kind of behaviour as they say; for the gentlewoman is young. And therefore, if you should 165 deal double with her, truly it were an ill thing to be offered to any gentlewoman, and very weak dealing.
Romeo.	Nurse, commend me to thy lady and mistress. I protest unto thee —
Nurse.	Good heart, and i'faith I will tell her as much. 170 Lord, Lord, she will be a joyful woman.
Romeo.	What wilt thou tell her, Nurse? Thou dost not mark me.
Nurse.	I will tell her, sir, that you do protest — which, as I take it, is a gentlemanlike offer. 175
Romeo.	Bid her devise Some means to come to shrift this afternoon,

143 *ropery*
vulgar, jesting

150 *flirt-gills*
loose women
151 *skains-mates*
cut-throat
companions

162–3 *lead her in a fool's paradise*
take advantage of
her, seduce her

167 *weak dealing*
contemptible
behaviour

	And there she shall at Friar Laurence' cell	
	Be shriv'd and married. Here is for thy pains.	
Nurse.	No truly, sir; not a penny.	180
Romeo.	Go to, I say you shall.	
Nurse.	This afternoon, sir? Well, she shall be there.	
Romeo.	And stay, good Nurse, behind the abbey wall.	
	Within this hour my man shall be with thee,	
	And bring thee cords made like a tackled stair,	185
	Which to the high topgallant of my joy	
	Must be my convoy in the secret night.	
	Farewell, be trusty, and I'll quit thy pains;	
	Farewell. Commend me to thy mistress.	
Nurse.	Now God in heaven bless thee. Hark you, sir.	190
Romeo.	What say'st thou, my dear Nurse?	
Nurse.	Is your man secret? Did you ne'er hear say,	
	Two may keep counsel, putting one away?	
Romeo.	I warrant thee my man's as true as steel.	
Nurse.	Well, sir, my mistress is the sweetest lady. Lord,	195
	Lord! When 'twas a little prating thing — O, there	
	is a nobleman in town, one Paris, that would fain	
	lay knife aboard; but she, good soul, had as lief see	
	a toad, a very toad, as see him. I anger her some-	
	times and tell her that Paris is the properer man,	200
	but I'll warrant you, when I say so she looks as pale	
	as any clout in the versal world. Doth not rosemary	
	and Romeo begin both with a letter?	
Romeo.	Ay, Nurse, what of that? Both with an 'R'.	
Nurse.	Ah, mocker! That's the dog's name, 'R' is for the	205
	—No, I know it begins with some other letter; and	
	she hath the prettiest sententious of it, of you and	
	rosemary, that it would do you good to hear it.	
Romeo.	Commend me to thy lady. [*Exit Romeo.*]	
Nurse.	Ay, a thousand times. Peter!	210
Peter	Anon.	
Nurse.	Before, and apace. *Exeunt.*	

185 *tackled stair* rope ladder
186 *topgallant* summit
187 *convoy* conveyance
188 *quit thy pains* reward your effort

198 *lief see* prefer to see

202 *clout in the versal world* cloth in the universe

207 *sententious* sentences (pithy sayings)

212 *apace* quickly

SCENE ANALYSIS

ACTION

1. Mercutio and Benvolio search for Romeo. Tybalt has sent a letter challenging Romeo to a duel and Mercutio worries that the lovesick Romeo will be no match for the duellist.
2. Mercutio expects Romeo to be melancholic and is surprised to find him in good humour. They jest with each other, exchanging puns.
3. The Nurse arrives with a message for Romeo and is ridiculed by Mercutio.
4. The Nurse attempts to discover Romeo's intentions and warns him not to trifle with Juliet's feelings.
5. Romeo sends a message to Juliet that she should meet him at Friar Lawrence's that afternoon to be married.
6. Romeo bribes the Nurse, telling her his man will bring a rope ladder to enable him to climb into Juliet's bedroom that evening.

THEMES

1. Again the theme is that of love. Mercutio mocks love, ridiculing legendary lovers and is delighted to find that Romeo is no longer 'groaning for love'.
2. The sincerity of love is dramatised in the scene when Romeo makes arrangements for Juliet to meet him to get married.

CHARACTERISATION

1. Mercutio is quick-witted and irreverent. His humour is lewd:

   > . . . For this drivelling love is like a great natural
   > that runs lolling up and down to hide his bauble in
   > a hole.

   His general attitude is sardonic and his humour ridicules the vanity and self-importance of others: 'Good Peter, to hide her face; for her fan's the fairer face', he says of the Nurse. When referring to Tybalt he says sardonically: 'More, than Prince of Cats. O, he's the courageous captain of compliments.'

2. In this scene Romeo shows himself to be witty and affable. He is capable of exchanging puns with Mercutio and of pacifying the Nurse. It appears that he can talk to anyone in his or her own language. This indicates that he is a sophisticated young man.

63

DRAMATIC EFFECT

1. The scene contains comic relief. It combines elements of farce (Peter's behaviour and the Nurse's pompous manner) with a comedy of ironic puns (the exchanges of Mercutio and Romeo).

2. The plot progresses, anticipating the marriage of the lovers, yet, with the reference to the rope ladder, emphasising the clandestine nature of their affair.

3. The spectre of the feud hangs over the scene. Tybalt's challenge will now contribute to the tension and suspense of the plot.

4. There is great movement and colour, with a number of characters coming and going. The rhythm of this scene, therefore, contrasts with the scenes before and after.

LANGUAGE

1. The language of Mercutio and Romeo is initially one of puns, playing with the ambiguity of words:

> Sure wit, follow me this jest now, till thou hast worn out thy pump, that when the single sole of it is worn, the jest may remain after the wearing solely singular. (Mercutio)

> O single-soled jest, solely singular for the singleness. (Romeo)

2. When the Nurse arrives, the language becomes more prosaic and colloquial. The images are concrete and the meanings more literal. Her direct language reflects her lowly station and her lack of education. This is in contrast to the sophisticated jesting of Romeo and Mercutio.

[SCENE V]

Introduction

This is quite a comic scene. Juliet is impatient to hear from Romeo and the Nurse teases her by delaying before telling her the news. It is a scene that reveals the intimate nature of the relationship between the Nurse and Juliet.

Enter JULIET.

Juliet.	The clock struck nine when I did send the Nurse,
	In half an hour she promis'd to return.
	Perchance she cannot meet him. That's not so.
	O, she is lame. Love's heralds should be thoughts
	Which ten times faster glides than the sun's beams 5
	Driving back shadows over lowering hills.
	Therefore do nimble-pinion'd doves draw Love,
	And therefore hath the wind-swift Cupid wings.
	Now is the sun upon the highmost hill
	Of this day's journey, and from nine till twelve 10
	Is three long hours, yet she is not come.
	Had she affections and warm youthful blood
	She would be as swift in motion as a ball:
	My words would bandy her to my sweet love,
	And his to me. 15
	But old folks, many feign as they were dead—
	Unwieldy, slow, heavy and pale as lead.

7 *nimble-pinion'd*
swift winged

14 *bandy*
toss (her)
16 *feign*
act, pretend

Enter NURSE [*and* PETER].

	O God she comes. O honey Nurse, what news?
	Hast thou met with him? Send thy man away.
Nurse.	Peter, stay at the gate. [*Exit Peter.*] 20
Juliet.	Now good sweet Nurse—O Lord why look'st thou sad?
	Though news be sad, yet tell them merrily,
	If good, thou sham'st the music of sweet news
	By playing it to me with so sour a face.
Nurse.	I am aweary, give me leave awhile. 25
	Fie, how my bones ache. What a jaunce have I!
Juliet.	I would thou hadst my bones and I thy news.
	Nay come, I pray thee, speak: good, good Nurse, speak.
Nurse.	Jesu, what haste. Can you not stay awhile?
	Do you not see that I am out of breath? 30
Juliet.	How art thou out of breath when thou hast breath

26 *jaunce*
walk, trudge

To say to me that thou art out of breath?
The excuse that thou dost make in this delay
Is longer than the tale thou dost excuse.
Is thy news good or bad? Answer to that. 35
Say either, and I'll stay the circumstance.
Let me be satisfied: is't good or bad?

Nurse. Well, you have made a simple choice. You know
not how to choose a man. Romeo? No, not he.
Though his face be better than any man's, yet his 40
leg excels all men's, and for a hand and a foot and a
body, though they be not to be talked on, yet they
are past compare. He is not the flower of courtesy,
but I'll warrant him as gentle as a lamb. Go thy
ways, wench, serve God. What have you dined at 45
home?

36 *stay the circumstance* wait for the details

38 *simple* foolish, stupid

Juliet.   *What says he of our marriage? What of that?*   line 48

Juliet. No, no. But all this did I know before.
What says he of our marriage? What of that?

Nurse. Lord, how my head aches! What a head have I:
It beats as it would fall in twenty pieces. 50
My back o' t'other side—ah, my back, my back!
Beshrew your heart for sending me about
To catch my death with jauncing up and down.

52 *Beshrew* Curse

Juliet.	I'faith I am sorry that thou art not well.
	Sweet, sweet, sweet Nurse, tell me, what says my
	love? 55
Nurse.	Your love says like an honest gentleman,
	And a courteous, and a kind, and a handsome,
	And I warrant a virtuous—Where is your mother?
Juliet.	Where is my mother? Why, she is within.
	Where should she be? How oddly thou repliest. 60
	'Your love says, like an honest gentleman,
	"Where is your mother?"'
Nurse.	O God's lady dear,
	Are you so hot? Marry, come up, I trow.
	Is this the poultice for my aching bones?
	Henceforward do your messages yourself. 65
Juliet.	Here's such a coil. Come, what says Romeo?
Nurse.	Have you got leave to go to shrift today?
Juliet.	I have.
Nurse.	Then hie you hence to Friar Laurence' cell.
	There stays a husband to make you a wife. 70
	Now comes the wanton blood up in your cheeks.
	They'll be in scarlet straight at any news.
	Hie you to church. I must another way
	To fetch a ladder by the which your love
	Must climb a bird's nest soon when it is dark. 75
	I am the drudge, and toil in your delight,
	But you shall bear the burden soon at night.
	Go. I'll to dinner. Hie you to the cell.
Juliet.	Hie to high fortune! Honest Nurse, farewell. *Exeunt.*

63 *hot*
eager
Marry, come up, I
trow
Come, come

73 *Hie*
Go

SCENE ANALYSIS

ACTION

1. Juliet awaits the return of the Nurse, wishing she could hurry her, impatient with the old woman.

2. The Nurse arrives and teasingly complains of tiredness and aching bones.

3. She mocks and praises Romeo, delaying the message, keeping Juliet in suspense.

4. The Nurse finally answers Juliet's impatience by telling her the plans for the wedding and saying that she must arrange for a rope ladder to allow the lovers to be together that night.

THEMES

1. There is a contrast between youth and age in this scene. The effect of the generation gap is evident in Juliet's impatience with the Nurse's slowness, which Juliet puts down to age.

2. It is obvious how time frustrates the lovers. When they are apart, time seems to drag.

3. The intensity of romantic love is felt in Juliet's impatience and frustration with the Nurse, and in her passionate need to know of Romeo's plans.

CHARACTERISATION

1. Juliet is headstrong and impatient in this scene. She initially tries to sweet-talk the Nurse:

> I would thou hadst my bones and I thy news.
> Nay come, I pray thee, speak: good, good Nurse, speak.

But her frustration and impatience cannot be concealed:

> Where is my mother! Why, she is within.
> Where should she be? How oddly thou replist.
> 'Your love says, like an honest gentleman,
> "Where is your mother?"'

It is obvious from their exchanges that Juliet is very much in love.

2. The Nurse teases Juliet in this scene and her behaviour is comical. She makes Juliet wait for the news and draws attention to her tiredness, again emphasising her own importance.

DRAMATIC EFFECT

1. This is another intimate scene. It reveals the closeness between Juliet and her Nurse.

2. The audience would find the exchanges amusing, knowing the content of Romeo's message and anticipating Juliet's delight when she hears the news. Consequently, the scene contains humour and comic relief.

3. This is the penultimate scene before the lovers meet for their marriage. It anticipates the wedding scene.

LANGUAGE

1. Juliet's opening speech is filled with vibrant imagery and powerful figures of speech. She imagines that lovers' communications should be like thoughts that transcend time. Her impatience with the Nurse's delay expresses itself in images, as she wishes that she could drive the Nurse onward with the power of language.

2. Once again, the Nurse's chosen expression is colloquial and quite literal, in contrast to Juliet's imaginative and poetic soliloquy.

[SCENE VI]

Introduction

The lovers meet at the Friar's cell to be married.

Enter FRIAR [LAURENCE] and ROMEO.

Friar L.	So smile the heavens upon this holy act		
	That after-hours with sorrow chide us not.		
Romeo.	Amen, amen, but come what sorrow can,		
	It cannot countervail the exchange of joy		4 *countervail* outweigh
	That one short minute gives me in her sight.	5	
	Do thou but close our hands with holy words,		
	Then love-devouring death do what he dare:		
	It is enough I may but call her mine.		12 *loathsome* sickening, hateful
Friar L.	These violent delights have violent ends		
	And in their triumph die, like fire and powder,	10	13 *confounds* defeats
	Which as they kiss consume. The sweetest honey		
	Is loathsome in his own deliciousness,		15 *Too swift arrives as tardy as too slow.*
	And in the taste confounds the appetite.		
	Therefore love moderately; long love doth so.		More haste, less speed.
	Too swift arrives as tardy as too slow.	15	

Enter JULIET *somewhat fast and embraces Romeo.*

Here comes the lady. O, so light a foot
Will ne'er wear out the everlasting flint.
A lover may bestride the gossamers
That idles in the wanton summer air
And yet not fall; so light is vanity.   20

Juliet.   Good even to my ghostly confessor.

Friar L.   Romeo shall thank thee, daughter, for us both.

Juliet.   As much to him, else is his thanks too much.

18 *gossamers*
spider's web
19 *wanton*
playful

Romeo.   . . . let rich music's tongue
Unfold the imagin'd happiness that both
Receive in either by this dear encounter.   lines 27–9

Romeo.   Ah, Juliet, if the measure of thy joy
Be heap'd like mine, and that thy skill be more   25
To blazon it, then sweeten with thy breath
This neighbour air, and let rich music's tongue
Unfold the imagin'd happiness that both
Receive in either by this dear encounter.

Juliet.   Conceit more rich in matter than in words   30
Brags of his substance, not of ornament.
They are but beggars that can count their worth,
But my true love is grown to such excess
I cannot sum up sum of half my wealth.

26 *blazon it*
broadcast it
27 *rich music's tongue*
Juliet's voice,
lover's words
30 *Conceit*
Imagination
30-34 *Conceit . . . my wealth.*
Real love does not need expression in words.

Friar L.   Come, come with me and we will make short
          work,   35
          For, by your leaves, you shall not stay alone
          Till holy church incorporate two in one.   [*Exeunt.*]

SCENE ANALYSIS

ACTION

1. Romeo is waiting in Friar Lawrence's cell to be married.
2. The Friar counsels patience and moderation, recognising that love which is too intense may not survive.
3. Juliet enters and Romeo declares how happy he is, asking her to respond in kind.
4. Juliet replies that true love cannot be put into words and that her happiness goes beyond description.
5. The Friar takes them away to be married.

THEMES

In many ways the marriage which is about to occur is the fulfilment of the lovers' dreams. The theme of love is again explored. However, it is balanced by the Friar's wise insights that 'violent delights have violent ends'. The commitment of the lovers is now realised.

CHARACTERISATION

1. The Friar again is wise in his insights and his advice.
2. Romeo is naïve in his belief that love can ignore all outside forces and even that it may defy death:

    Do thou but close our hands with holy words,

    Then love-devouring death do what he dare:

    It is enough I may but call her mine.

3. Juliet is more sensible in her manner and her vow of love. Although she is overcome by her feelings for Romeo, she knows that the reality of love must be more than just the idea of love:

Conceit, more rich in matter than in words

Brags of his substance, not of ornament.

DRAMATIC EFFECT

1. This is an intimate scene that invites the audience into the private world of the lovers. It is in contrast to the rhythmic street scenes and is more contemplative in mood.
2. There is suspense in the scene as, once again, Romeo tempts Fate. He defies death and feels that love can conquer all. However, the audience realises the foolishness of such impetuous remarks.
3. The scene moves towards a climax which takes place off-stage with the marriage of the lovers. This is unusual in that the climax is imagined rather than experienced by the audience.

LANGUAGE

1. The Friar uses figures of speech ('like fire and powder', 'the sweetest honey') and his words have a didactic intention.
2. Romeo's language is filled with hyperbole —

     . . . come what sorrow can,

     It cannot countervail the exchange of joy

     That one short minute gives me in her sight

   which mirrors his joy and belief that love can never be conquered.
3. Juliet's speech is more measured and realistic. She gently reminds Romeo that real love is beyond words and that it requires more 'substance' than mere description. This is a practical view, delivered in language that is logical and figurative (using metaphor: 'They are but beggars that can court their worth').

[ACT III]
[SCENE I]

Introduction

This scene is the turning point of the play. Tybalt finally confronts Romeo and their encounter results in death and banishment. The scene is filled with tension and suspense. It begins with Mercutio and Tybalt jeering each other and finishes with Romeo being exiled from Verona.

Enter MERCUTIO, BENVOLIO *and* MEN.

Ben.	I pray thee, good Mercutio, let's retire;	
	The day is hot, the Capels are abroad,	
	And if we meet we shall not 'scape a brawl,	
	For now these hot days is the mad blood stirring.	
Mer.	Thou art like one of these fellows that, when he	5
	enters the confines of a tavern, claps me his sword	
	upon the table and says 'God send me no need of	
	thee!' and by the operation of the second cup draws	
	him on the drawer, when indeed there is no need.	
Ben.	Am I like such a fellow?	10
Mer.	Come, come, thou art as hot a Jack in thy mood	
	as any in Italy; and as soon moved to be moody,	
	and as soon moody to be moved.	
Ben.	And what to?	
Mer.	Nay, and there were two such, we should have none	15
	shortly, for one would kill the other. Thou? Why,	
	thou wilt quarrel with a man that hath a hair more	
	or a hair less in his beard than thou hast. Thou wilt	
	quarrel with a man for cracking nuts, having no	
	other reason but because thou hast hazel eyes. What	20
	eye but such an eye would spy out such a quarrel?	
	Thy head is as full of quarrels as an egg is full of	
	meat, and yet thy head hath been beaten as addle	
	as an egg for quarrelling. Thou hast quarrelled with	

9 *drawer*
waiter

73

a man for coughing in the street, because he hath 25
wakened thy dog that hath lain asleep in the sun.
Didst thou not fall out with a tailor for wearing his
new doublet before Easter; with another for tying
his new shoes with old riband? And yet thou wilt
tutor me from quarrelling! 30

Ben. And I were so apt to quarrel as thou art, any man
should buy the fee simple of my life for an hour and
a quarter.

Mer. The fee simple! O simple!

32 fee simple absolute possession

Enter TYBALT, PETRUCHIO *and* Others.

Ben. By my head, here comes the Capulets. 35
Mer. By my heel, I care not.
Tyb. Follow me close, for I will speak to them.
Gentlemen, good e'en: a word with one of you.
Mer. And but one word with one of us? Couple it with
something, make it a word and a blow. 40
Tyb. You shall find me apt enough to that, sir, and you
will give me occasion.
Mer. Could you not take some occasion without giving?
Tyb. Mercutio, thou consortest with Romeo.
Mer. Consort? What, dost thou make us minstrels? 45
And thou make minstrels of us, look to hear nothing
but discords. Here's my fiddlestick, here's that shall
make you dance. Zounds, consort!
Ben. We talk here in the public haunt of men.
Either withdraw unto some private place, 50
Or reason coldly of your grievances,
Or else depart. Here all eyes gaze on us.
Mer. Men's eyes were made to look, and let them gaze.
I will not budge for no man's pleasure, I.

44 consortest keep company

47 fiddlestick sword
48 Zounds By God's wounds

Enter ROMEO.

Tyb. Well, peace be with you, sir, here comes my man. 55

Mer.	But I'll be hang'd, sir, if he wear your livery.
	Marry, go before to field, he'll be your follower.
	Your worship in that sense may call him 'man'.
Tyb.	Romeo, the love I bear thee can afford
	No better term than this: thou art a villain. 60
Romeo.	Tybalt, the reason that I have to love thee
	Doth much excuse the appertaining rage
	To such a greeting: villain am I none,
	Therefore farewell. I see thou knowest me not.
Tyb.	Boy, this shall not excuse the injuries 65
	That thou hast done me, therefore turn and draw.
Romeo.	I do protest I never injuried thee,
	But love thee better than thou canst devise
	Till thou shalt know the reason of my love.
	And so, good Capulet, which name I tender 70
	As dearly as mine own, be satisfied.
Mer.	O calm, dishonourable, vile submission:
	Alla stoccata carries it away! [*He draws.*]
	Tybalt, you rat-catcher, will you walk?
Tyb.	What wouldst thou have with me? 75

56 *livery* servants' uniform

62 *appertaining* accompanying

68 *devise* imagine

73 *Alla stoccata carries it away!* A thrust wins the day!

Mercutio.   *Tybalt, you rat-catcher, will you walk?*   line 74

Mer.	Good King of Cats, nothing but one of your nine
	lives. That I mean to make bold withal, and, as you

shall use me hereafter, dry-beat the rest of the eight.
Will you pluck your sword out of his pilcher by the
ears? Make haste, lest mine be about your ears ere 80
it be out.

Tyb. I am for you. [*He draws.*]

Romeo. Gentle Mercutio, put thy rapier up.

Mer. Come sir, your passado. [*They fight.*]

Romeo. Draw, Benvolio, beat down their weapons. 85
Gentlemen, for shame, forbear this outrage.
Tybalt, Mercutio! The Prince expressly hath
Forbid this bandying in Verona streets.
Hold, Tybalt! Good Mercutio!

> *Tybalt under Romeo's arm thrusts Mercutio in.*

A Follower. Away Tybalt. 90

> *Exit Tybalt [with his followers].*

Mer. I am hurt.
A plague o' both your houses. I am sped.
Is he gone, and hath nothing?

Ben. What, art thou hurt?

Mer. Ay, ay, a scratch, a scratch. Marry, 'tis enough.
Where is my page? Go villain, fetch a surgeon. 95

> [*Exit Page.*]

Romeo. Courage, man, the hurt cannot be much.

Mer. No, 'tis not so deep as a well, nor so wide as a
church door, but 'tis enough, 'twill serve. Ask for
me tomorrow and you shall find me a grave man.
I am peppered, I warrant, for this world. A plague 100
o' both your houses. Zounds, a dog, a rat, a mouse,
a cat, to scratch a man to death. A braggart, a
rogue, a villain, that fights by the book of arith-
metic—why the devil came you between us? I was
hurt under your arm. 105

Romeo. I thought all for the best.

Mer. Help me into some house, Benvolio,
Or I shall faint. A plague o' both your houses,

78 *use*
treat
dry-beat
thrash
79 *pilcher*
scabbard

84 *passado*
thrust

92 *sped*
finished

100 *peppered*
done for, killed

Mercutio.   . . . *A plague o' both your houses,*
       They have made worms' meat of me.   lines 108–09

       They have made worms' meat of me.
       I have it, and soundly too. Your houses!   110

                Exit [*Mercutio with Benvolio*].

Romeo.   This gentleman, the Prince's near ally,
       My very friend, hath got this mortal hurt
       In my behalf—my reputation stain'd
       With Tybalt's slander—Tybalt that an hour
       Hath been my cousin. O sweet Juliet,   115
       Thy beauty hath made me effeminate
       And in my temper soften'd valour's steel.

117 *temper*
temperament,
character

       Enter BENVOLIO.

Ben.	O Romeo, Romeo, brave Mercutio is dead,
	That gallant spirit hath aspir'd the clouds
	Which too untimely here did scorn the earth. 120
Romeo.	This day's black fate on mo days doth depend:
	This but begins the woe others must end.

Enter TYBALT.

Ben.	Here comes the furious Tybalt back again.
Romeo.	Again, in triumph, and Mercutio slain.
	Away to heaven respective lenity, 125
	And fire-ey'd fury be my conduct now!
	Now, Tybalt, take the 'villain' back again
	That late thou gav'st me, for Mercutio's soul
	Is but a little way above our heads,
	Staying for thine to keep him company. 130
	Either thou, or I, or both must go with him.
Tyb.	Thou wretched boy, that didst consort him here,
	Shalt with him hence.
Romeo.	This shall determine that.

They fight. Tybalt falls.

Ben.	Romeo, away, be gone,
	The citizens are up, and Tybalt slain! 135
	Stand not amaz'd. The Prince will doom thee death
	If thou art taken. Hence, be gone, away!
Romeo.	O, I am fortune's fool.
Ben.	Why dost thou stay?

Exit Romeo.

Enter Citizens.

Citizen.	Which way ran he that kill'd Mercutio?
	Tybalt, that murderer, which way ran he? 140
Ben.	There lies that Tybalt.
Citizens.	Up, sir, go with me.
	I charge thee in the Prince's name obey.

125 *respective lenity*
mild conduct

Enter PRINCE, MONTAGUE, CAPULET, *their* Wives *and* All.

Prince.	Where are the vile beginners of this fray?	
Ben.	O noble Prince, I can discover all	
	The unlucky manage of this fatal brawl. 145	
	There lies the man, slain by young Romeo,	
	That slew thy kinsman brave Mercutio.	

144 *discover*
reveal
145 *manage*
course

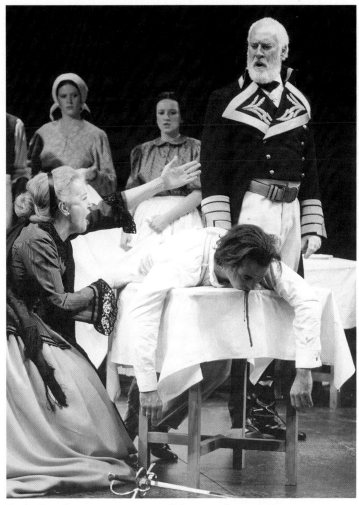

Lady Capulet.   *. . . Prince, as thou art true,*
For blood of ours shed blood of Montague. lines 150–151

Lady Cap. Tybalt, my cousin, O my brother's child!
O Prince, O husband, O, the blood is spill'd
Of my dear kinsman. Prince, as thou art true,   150

For blood of ours shed blood of Montague.

O cousin, cousin.

Prince. Benvolio, who began this bloody fray?

Ben. Tybalt, here slain, whom Romeo's hand did slay.

Romeo, that spoke him fair, bid him bethink   155

How nice the quarrel was, and urg'd withal

Your high displeasure. All this uttered

With gentle breath, calm look, knees humbly bow'd,

Could not take truce with the unruly spleen

Of Tybalt, deaf to peace, but that he tilts   160

With piercing steel at bold Mercutio's breast,

Who, all as hot, turns deadly point to point

And, with a martial scorn, with one hand beats

Cold death aside, and with the other sends

It back to Tybalt, whose dexterity   165

Retorts it. Romeo, he cries aloud

'Hold, friends! Friends part!' and swifter than his
    tongue

His agile arm beats down their fatal points

And 'twixt them rushes: underneath whose arm

An envious thrust from Tybalt hit the life   170

Of stout Mercutio; and then Tybalt fled,

But by and by comes back to Romeo,

Who had but newly entertain'd revenge,

And to't they go like lightning: for, ere I

Could draw to part them, was stout Tybalt slain,   175

And as he fell did Romeo turn and fly.

This is the truth, or let Benvolio die.

Lady Cap. He is a kinsman to the Montague.

Affection makes him false. He speaks not true.

Some twenty of them fought in this black strife   180

And all those twenty could but kill one life.

I beg for justice, which thou, Prince, must give.

Romeo slew Tybalt. Romeo must not live.

Prince. Romeo slew him, he slew Mercutio.

Who now the price of his dear blood doth owe?   185

156 *nice*
trivial
withal
in addition
159 *spleen*
temper

166 *Retorts*
Returns

170 *envious*
spiteful

Mont.	Not Romeo, Prince, he was Mercutio's friend;
	His fault concludes but what the law should end,
	The life of Tybalt.
Prince.	And for that offence
	Immediately we do exile him hence.

I have an interest in your hearts' proceeding;   190
My blood for your rude brawls doth lie a-bleeding.
But I'll amerce you with so strong a fine   *192 amerce*
That you shall all repent the loss of mine.   *punish*
I will be deaf to pleading and to excuses;
Nor tears nor prayers shall purchase out abuses.   195
Therefore use none. Let Romeo hence in haste,
Else, when he is found, that hour is his last.
Bear hence this body, and attend our will.   *199 pardoning*
Mercy but murders, pardoning those that kill.   *Exeunt.*   *a murder leads to more murders*

SCENE ANALYSIS

ACTION

1. Benvolio, on the streets of Verona with Mercutio, pleads with his friend to 'retire' from the streets as they are bound to meet Capulets and, as it is a hot day, tempers may flare.

2. Mercutio refuses to leave. Tybalt arrives with other Capulets. Mercutio mocks Tybalt, showing contempt for him.

3. Romeo arrives and Tybalt insults him, trying to goad him to fight.

4. Romeo ignores Tybalt's remarks because the Capulet is now his cousin.

5. Mercutio becomes angered by Romeo's indifference to the Capulet insults and challenges Tybalt to a fight.

6. While they are fighting, Romeo tries to separate them. Mercutio is stabbed and curses the Capulet and Montague houses before dying.

7. Romeo, distraught at the death of his friend, curses Juliet's love for having made him 'effeminate'.

8. Romeo follows Tybalt and avenges Mercutio's death, then realising he is 'fortune's fool' he flees.

9. Prince Escalus arrives and Benvolio is brought before him to explain what happened. Lady Capulet accuses him of lying.

10. The Prince exiles Romeo from Verona on punishment of death.

THEMES

This scene focuses on the damaging effects of the feud and the tragedy hatred brings. There is an inevitability about what happens when there is blind hatred. The love of Romeo and Juliet cannot remain untouched by outside influences and here their love is threatened by the feud.

CHARACTERISATION

1. Mercutio is an anarchic figure who has no regard for order and peace. His tone with Tybalt is sardonic and he deliberately tries to provoke him. He is impulsive and becomes offended by what he sees as Romeo's dishonourable ignoring of Tybalt's insults. Essentially, however, Mercutio is a figure of life and fun in the play. His death is a shock. Even when dying he jokes — 'Ask for me tomorrow and you shall find me a grave man'. His wit is irrepressible. Consequently, his cursing of the households is shocking and warns the audience of something dreadful to come.

2. Tybalt is a villainous character. He thrives on conflict and confrontation. His hatred requires satisfaction and he cares nothing for peace or the judgment of the Prince. His pursuit of Romeo is what leads to the tragedy. Tybalt, in many ways, personifies the feud and is an angel of death.

3. Benvolio once again is a voice of reason, aware of the dangers of fighting in the streets and trying to counsel peace.

4. Romeo, in this scene, is a moral young man. He initially displays great maturity. He refuses to be affected by Tybalt's badgering. He attempts to ignore the insults and to remain loyal to Juliet by not fighting his new relative. However, when Mercutio is killed, he blames himself. Consequently, driven by grief, and by honour and loyalty to his dead friend, he feels obliged to avenge Mercutio's death. His actions are impetuous and impulsive, leading to his downfall.

5. Lady Capulet is vindictive and vengeful. She accuses Benvolio of lying to protect Romeo and demands the full penalty of death from the Prince.

6. Montague is a concerned parent who attempts to appeal his son's punishment on the grounds that he only did what the state would have done.

7. Prince Escalus is a fair and just ruler. He must administer the law in an impartial fashion but he tempers that with mercy. In banishing Romeo, he imposes order and adheres to his previous warning that those involved in brawls must pay a penalty.

DRAMATIC EFFECT

1. This is the climax to the feud and a turning point in the play. What has been a play about life, love and youth now becomes a play about death.

2. The scene has plenty of colour and movement, with many characters coming on-stage and then leaving. This results in the scene having great vitality.

3. There is tension with the appearance of Tybalt; the audience recognise him as a dangerous individual and realise that his threats are serious.

4. The scene contains powerful suspense; the audience fear for those characters with whom they sympathise, such as Romeo and Mercutio.

5. The fights themselves provide great spectacle and allow the passions of the characters to be fully expressed.

6. The audience is aware of the role of Fate in the action and the scene allows them to anticipate the tragedy that is to come and places them as helpless and horrified observers.

LANGUAGE

1. Mercutio's jeering of Tybalt makes great use of puns and ambiguity. The tone is sardonic.

2. Tybalt's language is formal but also insulting. He patronises those around him and lacks the quick-witted banter of Mercutio.

3. Romeo's dialogue is initially courteous and sincere, attempting to placate Tybalt. Then his language becomes dark and passionate, filled with portents of doom.

4. The language of the Prince tends to be legalistic, focusing on judgment and decisions of authority.

[SCENE II]

Introduction

The scene opens with Juliet anticipating her wedding night with Romeo. The mood changes with the entrance of the Nurse who tells Juliet about Tybalt's death and Romeo's banishment. The atmosphere is one of despair and sadness.

Enter JULIET *alone.*

Juliet.	Gallop apace, you fiery-footed steeds,
	Towards Phoebus' lodging. Such a waggoner
	As Phaeton would whip you to the west
	And bring in cloudy night immediately.

Gallop apace, you fiery-footed steeds,
Towards Phoebus' lodging. Such a waggoner
As Phaeton would whip you to the west
And bring in cloudy night immediately.
Spread thy close curtain, love-performing night, 5
That runaway's eyes may wink, and Romeo
Leap to these arms untalk'd-of and unseen.
Lovers can see to do their amorous rites
By their own beauties; or, if love be blind,
It best agrees with night. Come, civil night, 10
Thou sober-suited matron, all in black,
And learn me how to lose a winning match
Play'd for a pair of stainless maidenhoods.
Hood my unmann'd blood, bating in my cheeks,
With thy black mantle, till strange love grow bold, 15
Think true love acted simple modesty.
Come night, come Romeo, come thou day in night,
For thou wilt lie upon the wings of night
Whiter than new snow upon a raven's back.
Come gentle night, come loving black-brow'd night, 20
Give me my Romeo; and when I shall die
Take him and cut him out in little stars,
And he will make the face of heaven so fine
That all the world will be in love with night,
And pay no worship to the garish sun. 25
O, I have bought the mansion of a love
But not possess'd it, and though I am sold,
Not yet enjoy'd. So tedious is this day
As is the night before some festival
To an impatient child that hath new robes 30
And may not wear them. O, here comes my Nurse.

Enter NURSE *with cords, wringing her hands.*

And she brings news, and every tongue that speaks

1 *fiery-footed steeds* horses of the run
2 *Phoebus* Sun god
waggoner driver
3 *Phaeton* Son of the sun who tried to drive his father's chariot and nearly set the earth on fire

25 *garish* too bright

But Romeo's name speaks heavenly eloquence.
Now, Nurse, what news? What hast thou there?
The cords that Romeo bid thee fetch?

Nurse.   Ay, ay, the

Juliet. Ay me, what news? Why dost thou wring thy hand

Nurse.   Ah weraday, he's dead, he's dead, he's dead!
We are undone, lady, we are undone.
Alack the day, he's gone, he's kill'd, he's dead.

Juliet. Can heaven be so envious?

Nurse.   Romeo can,   40
Though heaven cannot. O Romeo, Romeo,
Who ever would have thought it? Romeo!

Juliet. What devil art thou that dost torment me thus?
This torture should be roar'd in dismal hell.
Hath Romeo slain himself? Say thou but 'Ay'   45
And that bare vowel 'I' shall poison more
Than the death-darting eye of cockatrice.
I am not I if there be such an 'I',
Or those eyes shut that makes thee answer 'Ay'.
If he be slain say 'Ay', or if not, 'No'.   50
Brief sounds determine of my weal or woe.

Nurse. I saw the wound, I saw it with mine eyes
—God save the mark—here on his manly breast.
A piteous corse, a bloody piteous corse,
Pale, pale as ashes, all bedaub'd in blood,   55
All in gore-blood. I swounded at the sight.

Juliet. O break, my heart. Poor bankrupt, break at once.
To prison, eyes, ne'er look on liberty.
Vile earth to earth resign, end motion here,
And thou and Romeo press one heavy bier.   60

Nurse. O Tybalt, Tybalt, the best friend I had.
O courteous Tybalt, honest gentleman.
That ever I should live to see thee dead.

Juliet. What storm is this that blows so contrary?
Is Romeo slaughter'd and is Tybalt dead?   65
My dearest cousin and my dearer lord?

47 *cockatrice*
serpent with a
cock's head whose
look could kill

51 *weal*
welfare

54 *corse*
corpse

64 *contrary*
in opposite
direction

hen dreadful trumpet sound the general doom,

For who is living if those two are gone?

Tybalt is gone and Romeo banished.

Romeo that kill'd him, he is banished. 70

O God! Did Romeo's hand shed Tybalt's blood?

se. It did, it did, alas the day, it did.

iet. O serpent heart, hid with a flowering face.

Did ever dragon keep so fair a cave?

Beautiful tyrant, fiend angelical, 75

Dove-feather'd raven, wolvish-ravening lamb!

Despised substance of divinest show!

Just opposite to what thou justly seem'st!

A damned saint, an honourable villain!

O nature what hadst thou to do in hell 80

When thou didst bower the spirit of a fiend

In mortal paradise of such sweet flesh?

Was ever book containing such vile matter

So fairly bound? O, that deceit should dwell

In such a gorgeous palace.

Nurse. There's no trust, 85

No faith, no honesty in men. All perjur'd,

All forsworn, all naught, all dissemblers.

Ah, where's my man? Give me some aqua vitae.

These griefs, these woes, these sorrows make me old.

Shame come to Romeo.

Juliet. Blister'd be thy tongue 90

For such a wish. He was not born to shame.

Upon his brow shame is asham'd to sit,

For 'tis a throne where honour may be crown'd

Sole monarch of the universal earth.

O, what a beast was I to chide at him. 95

Nurse. Will you speak well of him that kill'd your cousin?

Juliet. Shall I speak ill of him that is my husband?

Ah, poor my lord, what tongue shall smooth thy name

When I thy three-hours wife have mangled it?

But wherefore, villain, didst thou kill my cousin? 100

67 *sound the general doom* announce judgment day

Juliet.   Shall I speak ill of him that is my husband?

line 97

That villain cousin would have kill'd my husband.

Back, foolish tears, back to your native spring,

Your tributary drops belong to woe

Which you mistaking offer up to joy.

My husband lives, that Tybalt would have slain,   105

And Tybalt's dead, that would have slain my husband.

All this is comfort. Wherefore weep I then?

Some word there was, worser than Tybalt's death,

That murder'd me. I would forget it fain,

But O, it presses to my memory   110

Like damned guilty deeds to sinners' minds.

Tybalt is dead and Romeo—banished.

That 'banished', that one word 'banished',

Hath slain ten thousand Tybalts: Tybalt's death

Was woe enough, if it had ended there.   115

Or if sour woe delights in fellowship

And needly will be rank'd with other griefs,

Why follow'd not, when she said 'Tybalt's dead',

Thy father or thy mother, nay or both,

Which modern lamentation might have mov'd?   120

But with a rearward following Tybalt's death,

'Romeo is banished': to speak that word

Is father, mother, Tybalt, Romeo, Juliet,

All slain, all dead. Romeo is banished,

There is no end, no limit, measure, bound,   125

In that word's death. No words can that woe sound.

Where is my father and my mother, Nurse?

Nurse.   Weeping and wailing over Tybalt's corse.

Will you go to them? I will bring you thither.

Juliet.   Wash they his wounds with tears? Mine shall be

    spent   130

When theirs are dry, for Romeo's banishment.

Take up those cords. Poor ropes, you are beguil'd,

Both you and I, for Romeo is exil'd.

He made you for a highway to my bed,

But I, a maid, die maiden-widowed.   135

Come, cords, come, Nurse, I'll to my wedding bed,

And death, not Romeo take my maidenhead.

Nurse.   Hie to your chamber. I'll find Romeo

To comfort you. I wot well where he is.

Hark ye, your Romeo will be here at night.   140

I'll to him. He is hid at Laurence' cell.

Juliet.   O find him, give this ring to my true knight

And bid him come to take his last farewell.   *Exeunt.*

SCENE ANALYSIS

ACTION

1. Juliet awaits nightfall and the consummation of her marriage to Romeo.
2. The Nurse tells Juliet the news of Tybalt's death.

3. Juliet initially curses Romeo but then rebukes the Nurse and herself for having blamed him.

4. Juliet is anguished about Romeo's banishment and feels that they will not now have a wedding night. However, thc Nurse says she will send Romeo to her.

THEME

The themes of love and hate are again in evidence in this scene. Juliet's love of Romeo is obvious in her opening soliloquy where she is impatient for nightfall. This hope is shattered by the hatred of the feud and what has happened on the streets.

CHARACTERISATION

1. Juliet is initially distraught at the news of Tybalt's death and her blame of Romeo is an impulsive reaction, from which she soon recovers. She is grief stricken by what has happened; banishment of Romeo is almost like death as he cannot be with her. Yet she regains her composure and shows courage and maturity in recognising that Romeo has survived, while Tybalt who would have killed him is dead.

2. The Nurse is sympathetic to Juliet's plight and is herself also grief stricken by the death of Tybalt. She tries to console Juliet by saying she will find Romeo and bring him to her. Yet, the Nurse does not really understand the love of the characters and is not in tune with Juliet's true feelings.

DRAMATIC EFFECT

Following the fight, this scene fully conveys the grief that results from what has happened. The tragic consequences of the feud are fully realised. It is a scene that elicits the sympathy of the audience for the plight of the lovers, who appear as innocent victims of their families' hatred. Fate also now seems to be playing a major role in the play, as it appears that the characters no longer control their own destinies.

LANGUAGE

1. Juliet's opening soliloquy is a kind of bridal song, anticipating her wedding night. The language is figurative and she tries, through the power of imagination, to conjure night. The opening images are, in effect, like a spell being cast. The language is another example of the lovers attempting to defy or change time and to create a parallel world of their own. The opening soliloquy is filled with wonderful images of night magically replacing day.

2. With the entrance of the Nurse, the language becomes more prosaic and colloquial, although the tone is passionate.

[SCENE III]

Introduction

Romeo has taken refuge with Friar Lawrence, awaiting the Prince's judgment. When he hears of his banishment he despairs, until the Friar counsels him on his good fortune.

Enter FRIAR [LAURENCE].

Friar L.	Romeo, come forth, come forth, thou fearful man.
	Affliction is enamour'd of thy parts
	And thou art wedded to calamity.

Enter ROMEO.

Romeo.	Father, what news? What is the Prince's doom?	
	What sorrow craves acquaintance at my hand	5
	That I yet know not?	
Friar L.	Too familiar	
	Is my dear son with such sour company.	
	I bring thee tidings of the Prince's doom.	
Romeo.	What less than doomsday is the Prince's doom?	
Friar L.	A gentler judgement vanish'd from his lips:	10
	Not body's death but body's banishment.	
Romeo.	Ha! Banishment! Be merciful, say 'death'.	
	For exile hath more terror in his look,	
	Much more than death. Do not say 'banishment'.	
Friar L.	Hence from Verona art thou banished.	15
	Be patient, for the world is broad and wide.	
Romeo.	There is no world without Verona walls	
	But purgatory, torture, hell itself;	
	Hence 'banished' is banish'd from the world,	
	And world's exile is death. Then 'banished'	20
	Is death, misterm'd. Calling death 'banished'	
	Thou cut'st my head off with a golden axe	
	And smilest upon the stroke that murders me.	

4 *doom* judgment

Friar L.	O deadly sin, O rude unthankfulness.	
	Thy fault our law calls death, but the kind Prince,	25
	Taking thy part, hath rush'd aside the law	
	And turn'd that black word 'death' to banishment.	
	This is dear mercy and thou seest it not.	
Romeo.	'Tis torture and not mercy. Heaven is here	
	Where Juliet lives, and every cat and dog	30
	And little mouse, every unworthy thing,	
	Live here in heaven and may look on her,	
	But Romeo may not. More validity,	
	More honourable state, more courtship lives	
	In carrion flies than Romeo. They may seize	35
	On the white wonder of dear Juliet's hand	
	And steal immortal blessing from her lips,	
	Who, even in pure and vestal modesty	
	Still blush, as thinking their own kisses sin.	
	But Romeo may not, he is banished.	40
	Flies may do this, but I from this must fly.	
	They are free men but I am banished.	
	And say'st thou yet that exile is not death?	
	Hadst thou no poison mix'd, no sharp-ground knife,	
	No sudden mean of death, though ne'er so mean,	45
	But 'banished' to kill me? 'Banished'?	
	O Friar, the damned use that word in hell.	
	Howling attends it. How hast thou the heart,	
	Being a divine, a ghostly confessor,	
	A sin-absolver, and my friend profess'd,	50
	To mangle me with that word 'banished'?	
Friar L.	Thou fond mad man, hear me a little speak.	
Romeo.	O, thou wilt speak again of banishment.	
Friar L.	I'll give thee armour to keep off that word,	
	Adversity's sweet milk, philosophy,	55
	To comfort thee though thou art banished.	
Romeo.	Yet 'banished'? Hang up philosophy.	
	Unless philosophy can make a Juliet,	

35 *carrion*
flies

38 *vestal*
virgin

52 *fond*
foolish

Displant a town, reverse a Prince's doom,

It helps not, it prevails not. Talk no more.   60

Friar L.   O, then I see that mad men have no ears.

Romeo.   How should they when that wise men have no eyes?   63 *estate*
situation

Friar L.   Let me dispute with thee of thy estate.

Romeo.   Thou canst not speak of that thou dost not feel.

Wert thou as young as I, Juliet thy love,   65

An hour but married, Tybalt murdered,

Doting like me, and like me banished,

Then mightst thou speak, then mightst thou tear thy
     hair

And fall upon the ground as I do now,

Taking the measure of an unmade grave.   *Knock.*   70

Friar L.   Arise, one knocks. Good Romeo, hide thyself.

Romeo.   Not I, unless the breath of heartsick groans

Mist-like infold me from the search of eyes   *Knock.*

Friar L.   Hark how they knock.—Who's there?—Romeo,
     arise,

Thou wilt be taken.—Stay awhile.—Stand up.   75

                                        Knock.

Run to my study.—By and by.—God's will,

What simpleness is this?—I come, I come.   *Knock.*

Who knocks so hard? Whence come you, what's your
     will?

Nurse.   [*Within.*] Let me come in and you shall know my
     errand.

I come from Lady Juliet.

Friar L.   Welcome then.   80

Enter NURSE.

Nurse.   O holy Friar, O, tell me, holy Friar,

Where is my lady's lord, where's Romeo?

Friar L.   There on the ground, with his own tears made drunk.

Nurse.   O, he is even in my mistress' case,

Just in her case. O woeful sympathy,   85

Piteous predicament. Even so lies she,

Blubbering and weeping, weeping and blubbering.
Stand up, stand up. Stand, and you be a man.
For Juliet's sake, for her sake, rise and stand.
Why should you fall into so deep an O?   *He rises*   90   *90 an O*
                                                                            lament, despair

Romeo.   Nurse.

Nurse.   Ah, sir, ah sir, death's the end of all.

Romeo.   Spak'st thou of Juliet? How is it with her?
Doth not she think me an old murderer
Now I have stain'd the childhood of our joy
With blood remov'd but little from her own?   95
Where is she? And how doth she? And what says
My conceal'd lady to our cancell'd love?   *97 conceal'd*
                                                                        not known as his
                                                                                   wife

Nurse.   O, she says nothing, sir, but weeps and weeps,
And now falls on her bed, and then starts up,
And Tybalt calls, and then on Romeo cries,   100
And then down falls again.

Romeo.   As if that name.
Shot from the deadly level of a gun,   *103 deadly level*
Did murder her, as that name's cursed hand   aim
Murder'd her kinsman. O, tell me, Friar, tell me,
In what vile part of this anatomy   105
Doth my name lodge? Tell me that I may sack   *106 sack*
The hateful mansion.   plunder

Friar L.   Hold thy desperate hand.
Art thou a man? Thy form cries out thou art.
Thy tears are womanish, thy wild acts denote
The unreasonable fury of a beast.   110
Unseemly woman in a seeming man,   *111 Unseemly*
And ill-beseeming beast in seeming both!   Unbecoming
Thou hast amaz'd me. By my holy order,
I thought thy disposition better temper'd.   *114 disposition*
Hast thou slain Tybalt? Wilt thou slay thyself?   115   character
And slay thy lady that in thy life lives,
By doing damned hate upon thyself?
Why rail'st thou on thy birth, the heaven and earth?
Since birth, and heaven, and earth all three do meet

In thee at once; which thou at once wouldst lose.   120

Fie, fie, thou sham'st thy shape, thy love, thy wit,   121 *wit*
                                                                          intelligence
Which, like a usurer, abound'st in all,

And usest none in that true use indeed

Which should bedeck thy shape, thy love, thy wit.

Thy noble shape is but a form of wax   125

Digressing from the valour of a man;

Thy dear love sworn but hollow perjury,

Killing that love which thou hast vow'd to cherish;

Thy wit, that ornament to shape and love,

Misshapen in the conduct of them both,   130   130 *conduct*
                                                                ruling,
Like powder in a skilless soldier's flask   management

Is set afire by thine own ignorance,

And thou dismember'd with thine own defence.   133 *dismember'd*
                                                           torn apart
What, rouse thee, man. Thy Juliet is alive,

For whose dear sake thou wast but lately dead.   135

There art thou happy. Tybalt would kill thee,

But thou slew'st Tybalt. There art thou happy.

The law that threaten'd death becomes thy friend

And turns it to exile. There art thou happy.

A pack of blessings light upon thy back;   140

Happiness courts thee in her best array;

But like a mishav'd and a sullen wench

Thou pouts upon thy fortune and thy love.

Take heed, take heed, for such die miserable.

Go, get thee to thy love as was decreed,   145

Ascend her chamber—hence, and comfort her.

But look thou stay not till the Watch be set,

For then thou canst not pass to Mantua,

Where thou shalt live till we can find a time

To blaze your marriage, reconcile your friends,   150   150 *blaze*
                                                                        proclaim,
Beg pardon of the Prince and call thee back,   announce

With twenty hundred thousand times more joy

Than thou wentst forth in lamentation.

Go before, Nurse. Commend me to thy lady

And bid her hasten all the house to bed,   155

Which heavy sorrow makes them apt unto.

Romeo is coming.

Nurse.   O lord, I could have stay'd here all the night

To hear good counsel. O, what learning is.

My lord, I'll tell my lady you will come.   160

Romeo.   Do so, and bid my sweet prepare to chide.

Nurse offers to go in and turns again.

Nurse.   Here sir, a ring she bid me give you, sir.

Hie you, make haste, for it grows very late.   *Exit.*

Romeo.   How well my comfort is reviv'd by this.

Friar L.   Go hence, good night, and here stands all your

state: 165   165 *all your state*
    your future

Either be gone before the Watch be set,

Or by the break of day disguis'd from hence.

Sojourn in Mantua. I'll find out your man,

And he shall signify from time to time

Every good hap to you that chances here.   170   170 *good hap*
    good luck

Give me thy hand. 'Tis late. Farewell, Good night.

Romeo.   But that a joy past joy calls out on me,

It were a grief so brief to part with thee.

Farewell.   *Exeunt.*

SCENE ANALYSIS

ACTION

1. Romeo is waiting in Friar Lawrence's cell to hear news of his sentence. When he hears of his banishment he is inconsolable.

2. Romeo draws his sword, despairing of seeing Juliet again, and threatens to kill himself.

3. The Friar reasons with Romeo and tells him to pull himself together, outlining the things he has to be thankful for: he won the duel, Juliet is alive, the threat of death has been replaced by exile, he can wait in Mantua until the time is right to return.

4. The Nurse presents Romeo with a ring that Juliet has asked her to give him as a sign of her love.

THEMES

The theme of Fate dominates this scene. Forces beyond Romeo seem to be controlling him. He is in despair until it is made clear to him that there is still much for which to be thankful. The shadow of the feud and the theme of love also pervade the scene.

CHARACTERISATION

1. The Friar is sensible in trying to restore Romeo's equilibrium. He chides him for not behaving like a man. However, he is sympathetic to Romeo's plight and is motivated by kindness and understanding. He is essentially optimistic in thinking that good will eventually prevail, and that time will find the lovers reunited and the families reconciled.
2. Romeo loses control of himself in this scene and appears desolate and despairing. He indulges in self-pity and is blind to the good fortune of having survived his fight with Tybalt. Both the Nurse and the Friar insist that, for Juliet's sake, he behaves like a man. It is eventually his love for her that strengthens his resolve and allows him to regain his composure.
3. The Nurse acts as messenger and is committed to helping Juliet. She is annoyed by Romeo's depression and she insists that he must think of Juliet's needs. It is obvious that her loyalty is to Juliet alone.

DRAMATIC EFFECT

1. This is a scene with great suspense and tension: it appears that the lovers are doomed to separation. Romeo seems to have lost control — his threat to kill himself is irrational and immature.
2. When the Nurse arrives, her knock is initially frightening, as it could be a threat to the safety of Romeo. The knocking sound therefore creates tension, while the entrance of the Nurse provides momentary relief.
3. The scene also has a dramatic intensity, with the hero of the play facing a conflict, not knowing what to do, and in the use of passionate and emotive dialogue.

LANGUAGE

The speeches in this scene are delivered at a high pitch, in a passionate tone. The Friar attempts to bring Romeo to his senses, while Romeo himself rants about his misfortune. The Friar's rhetorical speech, the longest in the play, develops logically in an effort to make Romeo realise how much is in his favour.

[SCENE IV]

Introduction

This is a transition scene. It provides an insight into how Tybalt's death has affected the Capulet household. Paris is still pursuing his marriage suit.

Enter CAPULET, LADY CAPULET *and* PARIS.

Cap.	Things have fallen out, sir, so unluckily	
	That we have had no time to move our daughter.	
	Look you, she lov'd her kinsman Tybalt dearly,	
	And so did I. Well, we were born to die.	
	'Tis very late. She'll not come down tonight.	5
	I promise you, but for your company,	
	I would have been abed an hour ago.	
Paris.	These times of woe afford no times to woo.	
	Madam, good night. Commend me to your daughter.	
Lady Cap.	I will, and know her mind early tomorrow.	10
	Tonight she's mew'd up to her heaviness.	

Paris offers to go in and Capulet calls him again.

Cap.	Sir Paris, I will make a desperate tender	
	Of my child's love. I think she will be rul'd	
	In all respects by me; nay, more, I doubt it not.	
	Wife, go you to her ere you go to bed,	15
	Acquaint her here of my son Paris' love,	
	And bid her—mark you me?—on Wednesday next—	
	But soft—what day is this?	
Paris.	Monday, my lord.	
Cap.	Monday! Ha ha! Well, Wednesday is too soon.	
	A Thursday let it be, a Thursday, tell her,	20
	She shall be married to this noble earl.	
	Will you be ready? Do you like this haste?	
	We'll keep no great ado—a friend or two.	
	For, hark you, Tybalt being slain so late,	
	It may be thought we held him carelessly,	25

Glosses:
1 *fallen out* happen
2 *move* persuade
11 *mew'd up* shut up
12 *desperate tender* bold offer
23 *ado* fuss
25 *carelessly* thought little of him

97

Being our kinsman, if we revel much.　　　　　　26 *revel*
celebrate

Therefore we'll have some half a dozen friends

And there an end. But what say you to Thursday?

Paris.　My lord, I would that Thursday were tomorrow.

Cap.　Well, get you gone. A Thursday be it then.　　30　32 *against*
for

Go you to Juliet ere you go to bed,

Prepare her, wife, against this wedding day.　　34 *Afore me*
Goodness

Farewell, my lord.—Light to my chamber, ho!

Afore me, it is so very late that we

May call it early by and by. Good night.　*Exeunt.*　35

SCENE ANALYSIS

ACTION

1. Capulet tells Paris that he has not had time to discuss the prospect of marriage with his daughter.
2. Lady Capulet promises Paris that she will convey Juliet's intentions to him early the following day.
3. Capulet then rashly promises his daughter's hand in marriage, telling Paris that he believes that she will follow his advice and that they shall be married the following Thursday.

THEMES

This scene obviously focuses on love and marriage. However, the kind of love here is very different to the passionate and all-consuming love of Romeo and Juliet. Here, the love of parents for their child is expressed in Capulet making the decision about his daughter's marriage. He feels that it is his responsibility as her father to arrange a good marriage for her; this, in a sense, is an expression of his love for her. Also, he feels that she will be guided by him. Paris's love is not evident. He approaches marriage as a contract, as Lady Capulet also sees it.

CHARACTERISATION

The Capulet parents are still in the throes of grief over the death of Tybalt. Capulet makes it clear that his household is upset. His intention in arranging Juliet's marriage is to put that tragedy behind them by securing his daughter's future and, therefore, can be regarded as honourable. Nonetheless, his actions are also convenient and one must question how heartfelt his grief over Tybalt's death actually is. He does, however, indicate that the marriage should be a small, private affair, in case people think they did not hold Tybalt in high regard.

DRAMATIC EFFECT

This scene drives the plot forward by introducing new complications for the lovers. It is essentially a brief, transition scene and, ironically, has Capulet arranging a marriage for his daughter while she is preparing for her wedding night. It develops suspense by presenting the audience with more information than that available to the characters and arouses their curiosity as to how Juliet will confront the new situation that is developing.

LANGUAGE

The language of this scene is straightforward. The dialogue is prosaic and the tone informal.

[SCENE V]

Introduction

This scene has two sections: it begins with Romeo reluctantly leaving Juliet's chamber after their wedding night; then it focuses on Juliet's rejection of Paris's proposal and her father's anger at her stubbornness. It is a scene in which the lovers see each other alone for the last time and have premonitions of disaster.

Enter ROMEO *and* JULIET *aloft at the window.*

Juliet.   Wilt thou be gone? It is not yet near day.
             It was the nightingale and not the lark
             That pierc'd the fearful hollow of thine ear.

Nightly she sings on yond pomegranate tree.

Believe me, love, it was the nightingale. 5

Romeo. It was the lark, the herald of the morn,

No nightingale. Look, love, what envious streaks

Do lace the severing clouds in yonder east.

Night's candles are burnt out, and jocund day   *9 Night's candles*

Stands tiptoe on the misty mountain tops. 10   The stars

I must be gone and live, or stay and die.

Juliet. Yond light is not daylight, I know it, I.

It is some meteor that the sun exhales

To be to thee this night a torchbearer

And light thee on thy way to Mantua. 15

Therefore stay yet: thou need'st not to be gone.

Romeo. Let me be ta'en, let me be put to death,

I am content, so thou wilt have it so.

I'll say yon grey is not the morning's eye,

'Tis but the pale reflex of Cynthia's brow. 20   *20 Cynthia*

Nor that is not the lark whose notes do beat   the moon

The vaulty heaven so high above our heads.

I have more care to stay than will to go.

Come death, and welcome. Juliet wills it so.

How is't, my soul? Let's talk. It is not day. 25

Juliet. It is, it is. Hie hence, begone, away.

It is the lark that sings so out of tune,

Straining harsh discords and unpleasing sharps.

Some say the lark makes sweet division.   *29 sweet division*

This doth not so, for she divideth us. 30   quick music

Some say the lark and loathed toad change eyes.

O, now I would they had chang'd voices too,

Since arm from arm that voice doth us affray,   *33 us affray*

Hunting thee hence with hunt's-up to the day.   frighten us

O now be gone, more light and light it grows. 35   *34 hunt's-up*

Romeo. More light and light: more dark and dark our woes.   morning greeting

Enter NURSE *hastily.*

Romeo.   *More light and light: more dark and dark our woes.*

                                                                    line 36

Nurse.	Madam.
Juliet.	Nurse?
Nurse.	Your lady mother is coming to your chamber.
	The day is broke, be wary, look about. [*Exit.*] 40
Juliet.	Then, window, let day in and let life out.
Romeo.	Farewell, farewell, one kiss and I'll descend.

He goes down.

Juliet. Art thou gone so? Love, lord, ay husband, friend,
I must hear from thee every day in the hour,
For in a minute there are many days.   45
O, by this count I shall be much in years
Ere I again behold my Romeo.

Romeo. Farewell.
I will omit no opportunity
That may convey my greetings, love, to thee.   50

Juliet. O think'st thou we shall ever meet again?

Romeo. I doubt it not, and all these woes shall serve
For sweet discourses in our times to come.

Juliet. O God, I have an ill-divining soul!
Methinks I see thee, now thou art so low,   55
As one dead in the bottom of a tomb.
Either my eyesight fails, or thou look'st pale.

Romeo. And trust me, love, in my eye so do you.
Dry sorrow drinks our blood. Adieu, adieu.

Exit.

Juliet. O Fortune, Fortune! All men call thee fickle;   60
If thou art fickle, what dost thou with him
That is renown'd for faith? Be fickle, Fortune,
For then I hope thou wilt not keep him long,
But send him back.

Enter LADY CAPULET.

Lady Cap.   Ho, daughter, are you up?

Juliet. Who is't that calls? It is my lady mother.   65
Is she not down so late, or up so early?
What unaccustom'd cause procures her hither?

She goeth down from the window.

Lady Cap. Why, how now Juliet?

[Enter JULIET.*]*

54 *ill-divining*
foreboding/seeing
evil

68 *how now*
how are you

102

Juliet.	Madam, I am not well.	
Lady Cap.	Evermore weeping for your cousin's death?	
	What, wilt thou wash him from his grave with tears?	70
	And if thou couldst, thou couldst not make him live.	
	Therefore have done: some grief shows much of love,	
	But much of grief shows still some want of wit.	
Juliet.	Yet let me weep for such a feeling loss.	
Lady Cap.	So shall you feel the loss but not the friend	75
	Which you weep for.	
Juliet.	Feeling so the loss,	
	I cannot choose but ever weep the friend.	
Lady Cap.	Well, girl, thou weepst not so much for his death	
	As that the villain lives which slaughter'd him.	
Juliet.	What villain, madam?	
Lady Cap.	That same villain Romeo.	80
Juliet.	Villain and he be many miles asunder.	
	God pardon him. I do with all my heart.	
	And yet no man like he doth grieve my heart.	
Lady Cap.	That is because the traitor murderer lives.	
Juliet.	Ay madam, from the reach of these my hands.	85
	Would none but I might venge my cousin's death.	
Lady Cap.	We will have vengeance for it, fear thou not.	
	Then weep no more. I'll send to one in Mantua,	
	Where that same banish'd runagate doth live,	
	Shall give him such an unaccustom'd dram	90
	That he shall soon keep Tybalt company;	
	And then I hope thou wilt be satisfied.	
Juliet.	Indeed I never shall be satisfied	
	With Romeo, till I behold him—dead—	
	Is my poor heart so for a kinsman vex'd.	95
	Madam, if you could find out but a man	
	To bear a poison, I would temper it—	
	That Romeo should upon receipt thereof	
	Soon sleep in quiet. O, how my hear abhors	
	To hear him nam'd, and cannot come to him	100

89 *runagate* vagabond, renegade

90 *dram* poison

97 *temper it* modify it, weaken it

	To wreak the love I bore my cousin	
	Upon his body that hath slaughter'd him.	
Lady Cap.	Find thou the means and I'll find such a man.	
	But now I'll tell thee joyful tidings, girl.	
Juliet.	And joy comes well in such a needy time.	105
	What are they, I beseech your ladyship?	
Lady Cap.	Well, well, thou hast a careful father, child;	
	One who to put thee from thy heaviness	
	Hath sorted out a sudden day of joy,	
	That thou expects not, nor I look'd not for.	110
Juliet.	Madam, in happy time. What day is that?	
Lady Cap.	Marry, my child, early next Thursday morn	
	The gallant, young, and noble gentleman,	
	The County Paris, at Saint Peter's Church,	
	Shall happily make thee there a joyful bride.	115
Juliet.	Now by Saint Peter's Church, and Peter too,	
	He shall not make me there a joyful bride.	
	I wonder at this haste, that I must wed	
	Ere he that should be husband comes to woo.	
	I pray you tell my lord and father, madam,	120
	I will not marry yet. And when I do, I swear	
	It shall be Romeo, whom you know I hate,	
	Rather than Paris. These are news indeed.	
Lady Cap.	Here comes your father, tell him so yourself,	
	And see how he will take it at your hands.	125

Enter CAPULET *and* NURSE

Cap.	When the sun sets the earth doth drizzle dew,	
	But for the sunset of my brother's son	
	It rains downright.	
	How now, a conduit, girl? What, still in tears?	
	Evermore showering? In one little body	130
	Thou counterfeits a bark, a sea, a wind.	
	For still thy eyes, which I may call the sea,	
	Do ebb and flow with tears. The bark thy body is,	
	Sailing in this salt flood, the winds thy sighs,	

129 *conduit*
fountain
131 *a bark*
a boat

	Who raging with thy tears and they with them,	135
	Without a sudden calm will overset	
	Thy tempest-tossed body. How now, wife?	
	Have you deliver'd to her our decree?	
Lady Cap.	Ay sir, but she will none, she gives you thanks.	
	I would the fool were married to her grave.	140
Cap.	Soft. Take me with you, take me with you, wife.	
	How? Will she none? Doth she not give us thanks?	
	Is she not proud? Doth she not count her blest,	
	Unworthy as she is, that we have wrought	
	So worthy a gentleman to be her bride?	145
Juliet.	Not proud you have, but thankful that you have.	
	Proud can I never be of what I hate,	
	But thankful even for hate that is meant love.	
Cap.	How, how, how, how? Chopp'd logic? What is this?	
	'Proud' and 'I thank you' and 'I thank you not'	150
	And yet 'not proud'? Mistress minion you,	
	Thank me no thankings nor proud me no prouds,	
	But fettle your fine joints 'gainst Thursday next	
	To go with Paris to Saint Peter's Church,	
	Or I will drag thee on a hurdle thither.	155
	Out, you green-sickness carrion! Out, you baggage!	
	You tallow-face!	
Lady Cap.	Fie, Fie. What, are you mad?	
Juliet.	Good father, I beseech you on my knees.	

She kneels down.

	Hear me with patience but to speak a word.	
Cap.	Hang thee young baggage, disobedient wretch!	160
	I tell thee what—get thee to church a Thursday	
	Or never after look me in the face.	
	Speak not, reply not, do not answer me.	
	My fingers itch. Wife, we scarce thought us blest	
	That God had lent us but this only child;	165
	But now I see this one is one too much,	
	And that we have a curse in having her.	
	Out on her, hilding.	

Marginal glosses:

136 *overset* overturn

144 *wrought* arranged for

149 *Chopp'd logic* Nonsense
151 *minion* hussy, minx

153 *fettle* make ready

157 *tallow-face* pale face

168 *hilding* good-for-nothing

Nurse.	God in heaven bless her.
	You are to blame, my lord, to rate her so.
Cap.	And why, my Lady Wisdom? Hold your tongue, 170
	Good Prudence! Smatter with your gossips, go.

169 *to rate*
to scold

171 *Smatter*
Chatter

Capulet.	*Hang thee young baggage, disobedient wretch!*
	I tell them what—get thee to church a Thursday
	Or never after look me in the face. *lines 160–162*

Nurse.	I speak no treason.
Cap.	O God 'i' good e'en!
Nurse.	May not one speak?
Cap.	Peace, you mumbling fool!
	Utter your gravity o'er a gossip's bowl,
	For here we need it not.
Lady Cap.	You are too hot. 175
Cap.	God's bread, it makes me mad! Day, night, work, play,
	Alone, in company, still my care hath been
	To have her match'd. And having now provided
	A gentleman of noble parentage,
	Of fair demesnes, youthful and nobly lign'd. 180
	Stuff'd, as they say, with honourable parts,
	Proportion'd as one's thought would wish a man—
	And then to have a wretched puling fool,
	A whining mammet, in her fortune's tender,
	To answer 'I'll not wed, I cannot love, 185

174 *gravity*
wisdom, opinion

184 *mammet*
doll, puppet
in her fortune's
tender
when a good
proposal is made

I am too young, I pray you pardon me!'
But, and you will not wed, I'll pardon you!
Graze where you will, you shall not house with me.
Look to't, think on't. I do not use to jest.
Thursday is near. Lay hand on heart. Advise.   190
And you be mine I'll give you to my friend;
And you be not, hang! Beg! Starve! Die in the streets!
For by my soul I'll ne'er acknowledge thee,
Nor what is mine shall never do thee good.
Trust to't, bethink you. I'll not be forsworn.   *Exit*   195

Juliet.   Is there no pity sitting in the clouds
That sees into the bottom of my grief?
O sweet my mother, cast me not away,
Delay this marriage for a month, a week,
Or if you do not, make the bridal bed   200
In that dim monument where Tybalt lies.

Lady Cap. Talk not to me, for I'll not speak a word.
Do as thou wilt, for I have done with thee.   *Exit.*

Juliet.   O God, O Nurse, how shall this be prevented?
My husband is on earth, my faith in heaven.   205
How shall that faith return again to earth
Unless that husband send it me from heaven
By leaving earth? Comfort me, counsel me.
Alack, alack, that heaven should practise stratagems   *209 strategems*
Upon so soft a subject as myself.   210   clever schemes
What sayst thou? Hast thou not a word of joy?
Some comfort, Nurse.

Nurse.   Faith, here it is.
Romeo is banish'd, and all the world to nothing
That he dares ne'er come back to challenge you.
Or if he do, it needs must be by stealth.   215
Then, since the case so stands as now it doth,
I think it best you married with the County.
O, he's a lovely gentleman.
Romeo's a dishclout to him. An eagle, madam,   *219 dishclout*
Hath not so green, so quick, so fair an eye   220   dishcloth

	As Paris hath. Beshrew my very heart,	
	I think you are happy in this second match,	
	For it excels your first; or, if it did not,	
	Your first is dead, or 'twere as good he were	
	As living here and you no use of him.	225
Juliet.	Speakest thou from thy heart?	
Nurse.	And from my soul too, else beshrew them both.	
Juliet.	Amen.	
Nurse.	What?	
Juliet.	Well, thou hast comforted me marvellous much.	230
	Go in, and tell my lady I am gone,	
	Having displeas'd my father, to Laurence' cell,	
	To make confession and to be absolv'd.	
Nurse.	Marry, I will; and this is wisely done.	*Exit.*
Juliet.	Ancient damnation! O most wicked fiend,	235
	Is it more sin to wish me thus forsworn,	
	Or to dispraise my lord with that same tongue	
	Which she hath prais'd him with above compare	
	So many thousand times? Co, counsellor.	
	Thou and my bosom henceforth shall be twain.	240
	I'll to the Friar to know his remedy.	
	If all else fail, myself have power to die.	*Exit.*

240 *twain*
separated

Scene Analysis

ACTION

1. The lovers must part as day arrives.
2. Juliet initially asks Romeo to stay, then realises he must leave.
3. Lady Capulet thinks the weeping Juliet is mourning the death of her cousin, Tybalt, and tells her she will have Romeo poisoned.
4. Juliet's mother also tells Juliet that she is to marry Paris on Thursday.
5. Juliet's father is furious when he hears that she will not marry Paris. He regards her as ungrateful and warns her that he will disown her if she does not agree to the marriage.

6. The Nurse is told to be quiet when she attempts to intervene. When Capulet has left, she advises Juliet to forget Romeo and marry Paris.

7. Juliet feels deserted and betrayed by the Nurse. She decides to confide in her no more.

8. Juliet resolves to ask the Friar for advice and help.

THEMES

1. The main theme here is the conflict between age and youth. The theme is that of the generation gap: parents not understanding their children.

2. The theme of love reaches an imaginative climax in this scene; Romeo is willing to stay and die if Juliet wishes it so, while Juliet insists that he goes when she is sure of his love and when she realises the danger he is in.

CHARACTERISATION

1. Romeo's devotion to Juliet is evident in this scene. He is willing to face death if she wishes it. He now listens to everything she says. In agreeing with her, it is a remarkable declaration of love.

2. Capulet should not be judged too harshly here. He is unaware of his daughter's marriage to Romeo. He sees an ungrateful daughter whose behaviour will humiliate him. His anger is a result of misunderstanding and frustration.

3. Lady Capulet is vengeful and the feud is kept alive in this vengefulness. She is selfish in her thirst for revenge and therefore is blind to what ails her daughter.

4. The Nurse here emerges as a weak and amoral character. Her attempt to take Juliet's side is half-hearted and she is easily silenced by the angry Capulet. Juliet's disappointment in and rejection of her means that the Nurse no longer enjoys the sympathy of the audience.

5. In this scene the audience witnesses how Juliet has been transformed by love. She stands up to her parents and rejects their suggestion of marriage to Paris. This is in direct contrast to her first appearance in the play (Act I Scene III) when she is willing to be guided by her mother's wishes. She now becomes heroic in her willingness to confront her destiny alone and to face death rather than betray Romeo.

DRAMATIC EFFECT

1. This is a scene filled with conflict and tension.

2. The contrast between age and youth, hate and love is evident.

3. The tragic dimensions of the play become obvious.

4. Characterisation is fully realised.

5. The pace of the scene, its rhythm, gradually gets faster as the scene progresses.
6. The scene's climax is full of passion and suspense.

LANGUAGE

1. The poetic language of the lovers, their attempt to deny the world of the feud, reaches a climax in this scene. There is a marriage of imagination.
2. The language of Juliet's parents is recognisable as the language of all parents. Capulet's ravings are almost clichéd. However, the tragedy of what is happening and his lack of awareness at his daughter's predicament lend a poignancy to his threats and dismayed rantings.

[ACT IV]
[SCENE I]

Introduction

This scene echoes that in which Romeo looked to Friar Lawrence for advice (Act III Scene IV). Now Juliet goes to the priest in despair at having to marry Paris and threatens suicide unless he can think of a scheme to help her. At this stage of the play, the inevitability of tragedy is becoming more obvious.

Enter FRIAR [LAURENCE] *and* PARIS.

Friar L.	On Thursday, sir? The time is very short.		
Paris.	My father Capulet will have it so,		
	And I am nothing slow to slack his haste.		3 *slack* delay
Friar L.	You say you do not know the lady's mind.		
	Uneven is the course. I like it not.	5	
Paris.	Immoderately she weeps for Tybalt's death,		
	And therefore have I little talk'd of love,		
	For Venus smiles not in a house of tears.		
	Now sir, her father counts it dangerous		
	That she do give her sorrow so much sway,	10	10 *sway* influence
	And in his wisdom hastes our marriage		
	To stop the inundation of her tears		
	Which, too much minded by herself alone,		
	May be put from her by society.		
	Now do you know the reason of this haste.	15	
Friar L.	I would I knew not why it should be slow'd—		
	Look sir, here comes the lady toward my cell.		

Enter JULIET.

Paris.	Happily met, my lady and my wife.
Juliet.	That may be, sir, when I may be a wife.

111

Paris.	That may be, must be, love, on Thursday next.	20
Juliet.	What must be, shall be.	
Friar L.	That's a certain text.	
Paris.	Come you to make confession to this father?	
Juliet.	To answer that, I should confess to you.	
Paris.	Do not deny to him that you love me.	
Juliet.	I will confess to you that I love him.	25
Paris.	So will ye, I am sure, that you love me.	
Juliet.	If I do so, it will be of more price	
	Being spoke behind your back than to your face.	
Paris.	Poor soul, thy face is much abus'd with tears.	
Juliet.	The tears have got small victory by that,	30
	For it was bad enough before their spite.	
Paris.	Thou wrong'st it more than tears with that report.	
Juliet.	That is no slander, sir, which is a truth,	
	And what I spake, I spake it to my face.	
Paris.	Thy face is mine, and thou hast slander'd it.	35
Juliet.	It may be so, for it is not mine own.—	
	Are you at leisure, holy father, now,	
	Or shall I come to you at evening mass?	
Friar L.	My leisure serves me, pensive daughter, now.—	
	My lord, we must entreat the time alone.	40
Paris.	God shield I should disturb devotion.	
	Juliet, on Thursday early will I rouse ye;	
	Till then, adieu, and keep this holy kiss. *Exit.*	
Juliet.	O shut the door, and when thou hast done so,	
	Come weep with me, past hope, past cure, past help!	45
Friar L.	O Juliet, I already know thy grief;	
	It strains me past the compass of my wits.	
	I hear thou must—and nothing may prorogue it—	
	On Thursday next be married to this County.	
Juliet.	Tell me not, Friar, that thou hearest of this,	50
	Unless thou tell me how I may prevent it.	
	If in thy wisdom thou canst give no help,	
	Do thou but call my resolution wise,	
	And with this knife I'll help it presently.	

21 *certain text*
the truth

40 *entreat*
ask for

47 *compass*
hunt
48 *prorogue*
put off

God join'd my heart and Romeo's, thou our hands;　55
And ere this hand, by thee to Romeo's seal'd,
Shall be the label to another deed,
Or my true heart with treacherous revolt
Turn to another, this shall slay them both.
Therefore, out of thy long-experienc'd time　60
Give me some present counsel, or behold:
Twixt my extremes and me this bloody knife
Shall play the umpire, arbitrating that
Which the commission of thy years and art
Could to no issue of true honour bring.　65
Be not so long to speak. I long to die
If what thou speak'st speak not of remedy.

57 be the label
the seal

64 commission
authority

Friar Laurence.   Hold, daughter, I do spy a kind of hope . . .　*line 68*

Friar L.　Hold, daughter, I do spy a kind of hope
Which craves as desperate an execution
As that is desperate which we would prevent.　70
If, rather than to marry County Paris,
Thou hast the strength of will to slay thyself,
Then is it likely thou wilt undertake
A thing like death to chide away this shame,
That cop'st with death himself to scape from it.　75
And if thou dar'st, I'll give thee remedy.

Juliet. O, bid me leap, rather than marry Paris,

From off the battlements of any tower,

Or walk in thievish ways, or bid me lurk

Where serpents are. Chain me with roaring bears,   80

Or hide me nightly in a charnel-house

O'ercover'd quite with dead men's rattling bones,

With reeky shanks and yellow chapless skulls.

Or bid me go into a new-made grave,

And hide me with a dead man in his shroud—   85

Things that, to hear them told, have made me tremble—

And I will do it without fear or doubt,

To live an unstain'd wife to my sweet love.

Friar L. Hold then. Go home, be merry, give consent

To marry Paris. Wednesday is tomorrow;   90

Tomorrow night look that thou lie alone.

Let not the Nurse lie with thee in thy chamber.

Take thou this vial, being then in bed,

And this distilling liquor drink thou off;

When presently through all thy veins shall run   95

A cold and drowsy humour, for no pulse

Shall keep his native progress, but surcease:

No warmth, no breath shall testify thou livest,

The roses in thy lips and cheeks shall fade

To wanny ashes, thy eyes' windows fall   100

Like death when he shuts up the day of life.

Each part depriv'd of supple government

Shall stiff and stark and cold appear, like death,

And in this borrow'd likeness of shrunk death

Thou shalt continue two and forty hours   105

And then awake as from a pleasant sleep.

Now when the bridegroom in the morning comes

To rouse thee from thy bed, there art thou, dead.

Then as the manner of our country is,

In thy best robes, uncover'd on the bier   110

Thou shall be borne to that same ancient vault

Where all the kindred of the Capulets lie.

*83 reeky shanks
and yellow
chapless skulls*
smelly legs and
fleshless skulls

97 native
own, natural

100 wanny
pale

*102 supple
government*
movement

In the meantime, against thou shalt awake,

Shall Romeo by my letters know our drift

And hither shall he come, and he and I   115

Will watch thy waking, and that very night

Shall Romeo bear thee hence to Mantua,

And this shall free thee from this present shame,

If no inconstant toy nor womanish fear

Abate thy valour in the acting it.   120

Juliet.   Give me, give me! O tell not me of fear.

Friar L.   Hold. Get you gone. Be strong and prosperous

In this resolve. I'll send a friar with speed

To Mantua with my letters to thy lord.

Juliet.   Love give me strength, and strength shall help

afford.   125

Farewell, dear father.   *Exeunt.*

113 against
in readiness
114 our drift
our plan

119 inconstant toy
whim
120 Abate
Lessen

SCENE ANALYSIS

ACTION

1. Paris tells Friar Lawrence that he and Juliet are to be married on Thursday. Her father, Paris says, hopes it will stop her grieving over the death of Tybalt.

2. The Friar questions the hastiness of the marriage.

3. Juliet arrives and the Friar asks Paris to give them time alone.

4. In the confessional, Juliet breaks down and pleads for help, but the Friar says that he is powerless.

5. Juliet takes out a dagger and threatens to kill herself rather than marry Paris.

6. The Friar suggests that if Juliet is willing to take her life rather than marry, then she may be willing to simulate death by means of a potion he will provide her with and which will keep her in a coma for forty-two hours, until he can send for Romeo to come and take her away.

THEMES

1. Juliet is willing to risk everything, even her life, for love. The romantic love of Romeo and Juliet, which is intense and all-embracing, is contrasted with the more formal and detached 'love' that is behind the arranged marriage.
2. The scene also alludes to the notion of Fate and Destiny. Juliet says 'what must be shall be' in resignation to Paris's comment about their upcoming nuptials. It is an ironic comment, but also a reference to Fate and the tragic inevitability of their destinies.

CHARACTERISATION

1. Juliet displays great courage in her willingness to be faithful to her husband. Love has provided her with a fierce determination and a strength of character.
2. The Friar is again an understanding and sympathetic confidante, although politically naïve in thinking that things can be resolved by means of coincidence. In a way, he is attempting to defy the stars.
3. Paris is well-meaning, but rather shallow. He does not consider Juliet's feelings and is more concerned with achieving his objective of marriage.

DRAMATIC EFFECT

1. There is an air of desperation about the scene. It echoes that in which Romeo also went to the Friar for advice and threatened to kill himself. The lovers are mirroring each other, which emphasises the sense of tragic inevitability and the mood of despair that has entered the play.
2. The scene increases the play's suspense and speeds up the rhythm. The audience awaits the moment when Juliet will take the potion, realising that her parents are unaware of her predicament. Also the brevity of the scene means that it has an abruptness to it that holds the audience and speeds up the pace of events.

LANGUAGE

1. Juliet's language complements that used by Romeo when he despaired of seeing her again. It is a language filled with hyperbole (exaggeration) and bold figures of speech.
2. The Friar's dialogue, on the other hand, is more prosaic and realistic. Because his is the voice of reason, he is less given to imaginative flights of fancy.

[SCENE II]

Introduction

This is another transition scene. The Capulets arrange a wedding feast and Juliet is reconciled with her father.

Enter CAPULET, LADY CAPULET, NURSE *and two or three* Servingmen.

Cap.	So many guests invite as here are writ.	
	[*Exit Servingman.*]	
	Sirrah, go hire me twenty cunning cooks.	2 *cunning* skilful
Ser.	You shall have none ill, sir, for I'll try if they can lick their fingers.	
Cap.	How! Canst thou try them so? 5	
Ser.	Marry sir, 'tis an ill cook that cannot lick his own fingers; therefore he that cannot lick his fingers goes not with me.	
Cap.	Go, be gone. *Exit Servingman.*	
	We shall be much unfurnish'd for this time. 10	10 *unfurnish'd* unprepared
	What, is my daughter gone to Friar Laurence?	
Nurse.	Ay, forsooth.	
Cap.	Well, he may chance to do some good on her.	
	A peevish self-will'd harlotry it is.	14 *peevish* irritable

Enter Juliet.

Nurse.	See where she comes from shrift with merry look. 15	15 *shrift* confession
Cap.	How now, my headstrong: where have you been gadding?	16 *gadding* wandering
Juliet.	Where I have learnt me to repent the sin	
	Of disobedient opposition	
	To you and your behests, and am enjoin'd	
	By holy Laurence to fall prostrate here, 20	

To beg your pardon. Pardon, I beseech you.
Henceforward I am ever rul'd by you.

She kneels down.

Cap.   Send for the County, go tell him of this.
      I'll have this knot knit up tomorrow morning.

Juliet.   I met the youthful lord at Laurence' cell,   25
      And gave him what becomed love I might,
      Not stepping o'er the bounds of modesty.

26 becomed fitting, proper

Cap.   Why, I am glad on't. This is well. Stand up.
      This is as't should be. Let me see the County.
      Ay, marry. Go, I say, and fetch him hither.   30
      Now afore God, this reverend holy Friar,
      All our whole city is much bound to him.

Juliet.   *. . . Pardon, I beseech you.*
Henceforward I am ever rul'd by you.   *lines 21–2*

33 closet room

Juliet.   Nurse, will you go with me into my closet,
      To help me sort such needful ornaments
      As you think fit to furnish me tomorrow?   35

Lady Cap.   No, not till Thursday. There is time enough.

Cap.   Go, Nurse, go with her. We'll to church tomorrow.

                         Exeunt Juliet and Nurse.

Lady Cap. We shall be short in our provision,

        'Tis now near night.

Cap.   Tush I will stir about,

        And all things shall be well, I warrant thee, wife.   40

        Go thou to Juliet, help to deck up her.

        I'll not to bed tonight, let me alone.

        I'll play the housewife for this once.—What ho!—

        They are all forth. Well, I will walk myself

        To County Paris, to prepare up him   45

        Against tomorrow. My heart is wondrous light   46 *Against*

        Since this same wayward girl is so reclaim'd.   *Exeunt.*   For

SCENE ANALYSIS

ACTION

1. Capulet makes arrangements for his daughter's wedding.
2. It is to be a large affair.
3. Juliet is reconciled with her father, apologising for her disobedience and saying she will be ruled by him in future.
4. Capulet is so pleased with his daughter's change of attitude that he brings the wedding forward to Wednesday.

THEMES

To an extent, this is a scene that shows the gap between the generations, their different attitudes and the level of misunderstanding between them. Capulet is unaware of where his daughter's real affections lie and of her thoughts.

CHARACTERISATION

1. Capulet is quite domineering at home. He orders the servants to do as he bids, he ignores his wife's objections to bringing the wedding forward a day and he is oblivious to Juliet's real feelings. He appears to be a selfish man, unlike the portrait that was given at the start of the play.

2. Juliet shows herself to be a mature, determined, faithful and shrewd young woman in this scene. She never betrays her true feelings or intentions and realises that it is necessary to reconcile herself with her father if her scheme is to work. Her love for Romeo is quite evident and her self-discipline is admirable.

DRAMATIC EFFECT

1. The fact that the marriage is brought forward a day puts pressure on Juliet and the Friar, which elicits the sympathy of the audience.
2. Suspense is built up in the scene as the audience wonder whether Juliet will be able to conceal her plans.
3. It is a short scene, with a good deal of activity, and this makes the pace of the play lively.

LANGUAGE

The language tends towards the colloquial, which emphasises the everyday nature of the domestic setting.

[SCENE III]

Introduction

In this very powerful scene, Juliet retires to her room the night before her wedding to Paris. She is completely isolated and considers the dangers in taking the Friar's potion.

Enter JULIET *and* NURSE.

Juliet.	Ay, those attires are best. But, gentle Nurse,	
	I pray thee leave me to myself tonight,	
	For I have need of many orisons	3 *orisons*
	To move the heavens to smile upon my state,	prayers
	Which, well thou know'st, is cross and full of sin. 5	5 *cross*
		wayward

Enter LADY CAPULET.

Lady Cap.	What, are you busy, ho? Need you my help?
Juliet.	No, madam, we have cull'd such necessaries
	As are behoveful for our state tomorrow.
	So please you, let me now be left alone
	And let the Nurse this night sit up with you, 10
	For I am sure you have your hands full all
	In this so sudden business.
Lady Cap.	Good night.
	Get thee to bed and rest, for thou hast need.

7 cull'd
chosen
8 behoveful
needed, necessary

Exeunt [Lady Capulet and Nurse].

Juliet.   *I have a faint cold fear thrills through my veins*
That almost freezes up the heat of life.

lines 15–16

Juliet.	Farewell. God knows when we shall meet again.
	I have a faint cold fear thrills through my veins 15
	That almost freezes up the heat of life.
	I'll call them back again to comfort me.
	—Nurse!—What should she do here?
	My dismal scene I needs must act alone.

Come vial.   20

What if this mixture do not work at all?

Shall I be married then tomorrow morning?

No! No! This shall forbid it. Lie thou there.

[*She lays down a knife.*]

What if it be a poison which the Friar

Subtly hath minister'd to have me dead,   25

Lest in this marriage he should be dishonour'd,

Because he married me before to Romeo?

I fear it is. And yet methinks it should not,

For he hath still been tried a holy man.

How if, when I am laid into the tomb,   30

I wake before the time that Romeo

Come to redeem me? There's a fearful point!

Shall I not then be stifled in the vault,

To whose foul mouth no healthsome air breathes in,

And there die strangled ere my Romeo comes?   35

Or, if I live, is it not very like,

The horrible conceit of death and night

Together with the terror of the place,

As in a vault, an ancient receptacle

Where for this many hundred years the bones   40

Of all my buried ancestors are pack'd,

Where bloody Tybalt yet but green in earth

Lies festering in his shroud; where, as they say,

At some hours in the night spirits resort—

Alack, alack! Is it not like that I   45

So early waking, what with loathsome smells,

And shrieks like mandrakes torn out of the earth,

That living mortals, hearing them, run mad—

O, if I wake, shall I not be distraught,

Environed with all these hideous fears,   50

And madly play with my forefathers' joints,

And pluck the mangled Tybalt from his shroud,

And, in this rage, with some great kinsman's bone

As with a club dash out my desperate brains?

29 *still been tried*
always proved to
be

37 *conceit*
image, thought

47 *mandrakes*
a plant which
screams when
uprooted and
sends the person
mad
49 *distraught*
driven mad
50 *Environed*
Surrounded

122

> O look, methinks I see my cousin's ghost   55
> Seeking out Romeo that did spit his body
> Upon a rapier's point! Stay, Tybalt, stay!
> Romeo, Romeo, Romeo, here's drink! I drink to thee!
>
> *She falls upon her bed within the curtains.*

SCENE ANALYSIS

ACTION

1. Juliet is preparing to retire and asks the Nurse and her mother to leave her alone to prepare for the wedding.
2. Juliet now has a nervous feeling and, sensing disaster, she craves human companionship.
3. She runs through the possibilities: she worries that the potion will fail and puts a dagger beside her; she is afraid that the potion may be poison; she is concerned about suffocation, waking up in a strange place, losing her mind; she worries that Tybalt will rise from the grave to avenge himself on Romeo.
4. She drinks from the vial containing the potion and falls on her bed.

THEMES

This scene concerns the sacrifices that love entails and demands. It also reintroduces the topic of the feud with references to Tybalt and the banished Romeo. Finally, the spectre of death and Fate hangs over the scene.

CHARACTERISATION

Juliet shows tremendous courage in this scene. Her strength of character is evident in her resolve to do everything in her power to be reunited with Romeo. She rejects the hatred of the world in which she lives and risks death to escape it. Her anticipation of the horrors of the vault in which she is to be buried emphasises her bravery. Her role of tragic heroine is fully defined in the moment when she confronts her fears and yet takes the poison.

DRAMATIC EFFECT

1. This is a scene filled with suspense and tension. Juliet has a dilemma and struggles with her decision, which is the basis of conflict in the scene.
2. The horrors of the tomb are conjured up through Juliet's imagination, which elicits the sympathy of the audience for the heroine who is alone on stage.
3. Juliet's sense of despair and alienation are fully evoked in the scene, with the audience horrified by the actions to which she is driven.
4. The audience is aware that Juliet has not been able to warn the Friar about her father's change in plans and that this will affect the timing of his arrangements to contact Romeo, so they anticipate things going horribly wrong.

LANGUAGE

Although this is an intense scene, filled with nightmarish images, Juliet's soliloquy is delivered in simple diction. While she makes use of some figures of speech, the images are sensual and concrete. There is little difficulty with the words themselves: the language is direct, conversational and intimate, which makes Juliet's terrifying ordeal immediately accessible to the audience.

[SCENE IV]

Introduction

Arrangements for the wedding feast continue.

Enter **LADY CAPULET** and **NURSE**.

Lady Cap. Hold, take these keys and fetch more spices, Nurse.
Nurse. They call for dates and quinces in the pastry.

> 2 *quinces*
> a bitter fruit
> *pastry*
> kitchen

Enter **CAPULET**.

Cap. Come, stir, stir, stir, the second cock hath crow'd!
The curfew bell hath rung, 'tis three o'clock.

Look to the bak'd meats, good Angelica: 5
Spare not for cost.

Nurse.   Go, you cot-quean, go,

6 *cot-quean*
man doing a
woman's work

Get you to bed. Faith, you'll be sick tomorrow
For this night's watching.

Cap.   No, not a whit. What, I have watch'd ere now
All night for lesser cause, and ne'er been sick.   10

Lady Cap. Ay, you have been a mouse-hunt in your time;
But I will watch you from such watching now.

11 *mouse-hunt*
a prowler,
womaniser

          Exeunt Lady Capulet and Nurse.

Cap.   A jealous-hood, a jealous-hood!

13 *jealous-hood*
jealous woman

          Enter three or four Servingmen *with spits and logs
          and baskets.*

          Now fellow, what is there?

1 Ser. Things for the cook, sir, but I know not what.
Cap.   Make haste, make haste!   [*Exit 1 Servingman.*]
          —Sirrah, fetch drier logs!   15
Call Peter, he will show thee where they are.
2 Ser. I have a head, sir, that will find out logs
And never trouble Peter for the matter.
Cap.   Mass and well said! A merry whoreson, ha.
Thou shalt be loggerhead!   [*Exit 2 Servingman.*]
          —Good faith! 'Tis day!   20
          Play music.

The County will be here with music straight,
For so he said he would. I hear him near.
Nurse! Wife! What ho! What, Nurse I say!

          Enter NURSE.

Go waken Juliet, go, and trim her up.
I'll go and chat with Paris. Hie, make haste,   25
Make haste! The bridegroom he is come already.
Make haste I say.   [*Exeunt Capulet and Servingmen.*]

SCENE ANALYSIS

ACTION

The last-minute details concerning the marriage, which is only six hours away, are being attended to: food, musicians and heat.

THEMES

The scene focuses on the wedding and the arranged marriage, referring to ritual, social status and the notion of marriage as a celebration and a contract.

CHARACTERISATION

Capulet rushes around the house giving orders, enjoying the excitement of the impending marriage.

DRAMATIC EFFECT

There is suspense as the audience await the discovery of the dead or drugged body of Juliet. The audience realise how blind Capulet is and recognise the irony of the situation. The scene has great life and movement as the servants and parents bustle around the house. Essentially, the function of this transition scene is to provide relief and to build suspense.

LANGUAGE

The language is prosaic and colloquial.

[SCENE V]

Introduction

In this scene, the Nurse is unable to arouse Juliet and she is taken for dead.
The Capulet household is devastated and a mood of gloom prevails.

[*Nurse goes to curtains.*]

Nurse.   Mistress! What, mistress! Juliet! Fast, I warrant her,
        she.

1 *Fast*
Asleep

Why, lamb, why, lady, fie! You slug-abed!

Why, love I say! Madam! Sweetheart! Why, bride!

What, not a word? You take your pennyworths now.

Sleep for a week; for the next night, I warrant,   5

The County Paris hath set up his rest

That you shall rest but little! God forgive me!

Marry and amen. How sound is she asleep!

I needs must wake her. Madam, madam, madam!

Ay, let the County take you in your bed,   10

He'll fright you up, i'faith. Will it not be?

What, dress'd, and in your clothes, and down again?

I must needs wake you. Lady! Lady! Lady!

Alas, alas! Help, help! My lady's dead!

O weraday that ever I was born.   15

Some aqua vitae, ho! My lord! My lady!

Enter LADY CAPULET.

Lady Cap. What noise is here?

Nurse.   O lamentable day!

Lady Cap. What is the matter?

Nurse.   Look, look! O heavy day!

Lady Cap. O me, O me, My child, my only life.

Revive, look up, or I will die with thee.   20

Help, help! Call help!

Enter CAPULET.

Cap.   For shame, bring Juliet forth, her lord is come.

Nurse.   She's dead, deceas'd! She's dead! Alack the day!

Lady Cap. Alack the day! She's dead, she's dead, she's dead!

Cap.   Ha! Let me see her. Out alas. She's cold,   25

Her blood is settled and her joints are stiff.

Life and these lips have long been separated.

Death lies on her like an untimely frost

Upon the sweetest flower of all the field.

Nurse.   O lamentable day!

Lady Cap.	O woeful time!	30
Cap.	Death, that hath ta'en her hence to make me wail	
	Ties up my tongue and will not let me speak.	

Enter FRIAR [LAURENCE] *and* PARIS *and* MUSICIANS.

Friar L.	Come, is the bride ready to go to church?	
Cap.	Ready to go, but never to return.	
	O son, the night before thy wedding day	35
	Hath Death lain with thy wife. There she lies,	
	Flower as she was, deflowered by him.	
	Death is my son-in-law, Death is my heir.	
	My daughter he hath wedded. I will die,	
	And leave him all: life, living, all is Death's.	40
Paris.	Have I thought long to see this morning's face,	
	And doth it give me such a sight as this?	
Lady Cap.	Accurs'd, unhappy, wretched, hateful day.	
	Most miserable hour that e'er time saw	
	In lasting labour of his pilgrimage.	45
	But one, poor one, one poor and loving child,	
	But one thing to rejoice and solace in,	

47 *solace*
comfort

Paris.   *Have I thought long to see this morning's face,*
And doth it give me such a sight as this?   lines 41–2

	And cruel Death hath catch'd it from my sight.
Nurse.	O woe! O woeful, woeful, woeful day.
	Most lamentable day. Most woeful day 50
	That ever, ever I did yet behold.
	O day, O day, O day, O hateful day.
	Never was seen so black a day as this.
	O woeful day, O woeful day.
Paris.	Beguil'd, divorced, wronged, spited, slain. 55
	Most detestable Death, by thee beguil'd,
	By cruel, cruel thee quite overthrown.
	O love! O life! Not life, but love in death!
Cap.	Despis'd, distressed, hated, martyr'd, kill'd.
	Uncomfortable time, why cam'st thou now 60
	To murder, murder our solemnity?
	O child, O child! My soul and not my child,
	Dead art thou. Alack, my child is dead,
	And with my child my joys are buried.
Friar L.	Peace, ho, for shame. Confusion's cure lives not 65
	In these confusions. Heaven and yourself
	Had part in this fair maid, now heaven hath all,
	And all the better is it for the maid.
	Your part in her you could not keep from death,
	But heaven keeps his part in eternal life. 70
	The most you sought was her promotion,
	For 'twas your heaven she should be advanc'd,
	And weep ye now, seeing she is advanc'd
	Above the clouds, as high as heaven itself?
	O, in this love you love your child so ill 75
	That you run mad, seeing that she is well.
	She's not well married that lives married long,
	But she's best married that dies married young.
	Dry up your tears, and stick your rosemary
	On this fair corse, and, as the custom is, 80
	All in her best array bear her to church.
	For though fond nature bids us all lament,
	Yet nature's tears are reason's merriment.

55 *Beguil'd*
Fooled, deceived

59 *Despis'd*
Hated by fate

61 *solemnity*
ceremony

65 *Confusion*
Destruction

70 *his part*
her soul

82 *fond nature*
natural feelings

Cap.	All things that we ordained festival
	Turn from their office to black funeral: 85
	Our instruments to melancholy bells,
	Our wedding cheer to a sad burial feast;
	Our solemn hymns to sullen dirges change,
	Our bridal flowers serve for a buried corse,
	And all things change them to the contrary. 90
Friar L.	Sir, go you in, and madam, go with him,
	And go, Sir Paris. Every one prepare
	To follow this fair corse unto her grave.
	The heavens do lour upon you for some ill;
	Move them no more by crossing their high will. 95

      Exeunt all but the Nurse and Musicians, casting rosemary
              on Juliet and shutting the curtains.

1 Mus.	Faith, we may put up our pipes and be gone.
Nurse.	Honest good fellows, ah put up, put up,
	For well you know this is a pitiful case.
1 Mus.	Ay, by my troth, the case may be amended.

                                    Exit Nurse.

                    Enter PETER.

Peter.	Musicians, O musicians, 'Heart's ease', 'Heart's 100 ease'! O, and you will have me live, play 'Heart's ease'.
1 Mus.	Why 'Heart's ease'?
Peter.	O musicians, because my heart itself plays 'My heart is full'. O play me some merry dump to 105 comfort me.
1 Mus.	Not a dump we! 'Tis no time to play now.
Peter.	You will not then?
1 Mus.	No.
Peter.	I will then give it you soundly. 110
1 Mus.	What will you give us?
Peter.	No money, on my faith, but the gleek! I will give you the minstrel.
1 Mus.	Then will I give you the serving-creature.

83 *reason's merriment* laughable when considered logically

112 *gleek* jest, gibe

Peter.	Then will I lay the serving-creature's dagger on 115 your pate. I will carry no crotchets. I'll re you, I'll fa you. Do you note me?
1 Mus.	And you re us and fa us, you note us.
2 Mus.	Pray you put up your dagger and put out your wit.
Peter.	Then have at you with my wit. I will dry-beat you 120 with an iron wit, and put up my iron dagger. Answer me like me.

       'When griping griefs the heart doth wound,

       And doleful dumps the mind oppress,

       Then music with her silver sound'— 125

	Why 'silver sound'? Why 'music with her silver sound'? What say you, Simon Catling?
1 Mus.	Marry, sir, because silver hath a sweet sound.
Peter.	Prates. What say you, Hugh Rebeck?
2 Mus.	I say 'silver sound' because musicians sound for 130 silver.
Peter.	Prates too. What say you, James Soundpost?
3 Mus.	Faith, I know not what to say.
Peter.	O, I cry you mercy, you are the singer. I will say for you. It is 'music with her silver sound' because 135 musicians have no gold for sounding.

       'Then music with her silver sound

       With speedy help doth lend redress.'   *Exit.*

1 Mus.	What a pestilent knave is this same.
2 Mus.	Hang him, Jack. Come, we'll in here, tarry for 140 the mourners, and stay dinner. *Exeunt.*

116 pate
head
carry no crotchets
put up with none
of your nonsense

127 Simon Catling
cat gut (usual to
musicians)
129 Hugh Rebeck
fiddle

*132 James
Soundpost*
wooden bridge on
fiddle
*134 I cry you
mercy*
I beg your
pardon

SCENE ANALYSIS

ACTION

1. The Nurse goes to arouse Juliet and believes that she is dead. She calls Juliet's parents.

2. Lady Capulet is shocked when she enters to find her daughter apparently dead. Then Capulet comes in and mourns his daughter.
3. The Friar arrives with Paris and the musicians and is told of Juliet's death.
4. Friar Lawrence restores calm with the assurance that Juliet has found happiness in heaven. He advises an early burial, suggesting they should all follow her to the crypt.
5. Capulet orders that everything arranged for the wedding feast should now become the trappings of a funeral.
6. Peter and the musicians have a difference in opinion and a banter develops between them, with him requesting music and them refusing it.

THEMES

The themes of Fate, feuding and love frustrated are all present in the scene. There is also the added theme of appearance and reality.

CHARACTERISATION

1. Capulet is devastated by the death of his daughter, which is in contrast to the portrait of the man who imposed order on his house and demanded his daughter's obedience. This image recalls his opening conversation when he resisted an immediate marriage of his daughter to Paris because he did not want to lose her at such a young age.
2. Lady Capulet's reaction to the death of her daughter is more conventional and even a little selfish. We cannot help feeling that her upset is caused not only by Juliet's death but also by the frustration of her desire for a marriage that would have united two powerful families. Her husband's grief has a more truthful ring.
3. The Friar is calm because he is aware that his plan is working. Surrounded by the hysterical reactions of the Capulet household, he points out the futility of succumbing to grief. He uses the occasion to moralise, and points out that the Capulets had sought Juliet's 'promotion' and that now she is promoted as high as she may go.
4. The Nurse is genuinely upset that Juliet is dead and appears inconsolable. It is important to note that she failed Juliet through her own character flaws rather than because of conscious betrayal. The fact that she was devoted to Juliet and loved her very much is obvious in her reaction to her death.

DRAMATIC EFFECT

1. The scene has an air of tragedy to it. Yet, the audience realise that the appearance of death is not the reality and that the real heartbreak has still to come.

2. The scene brings to an abrupt halt the preparations for the wedding. There is a sudden shift in mood and rhythm.

3. The scene is dramatic in the variations on the emotion of grief that are displayed. Each of the characters feels a need to respond in an appropriate manner and that underlines the conventional and almost shallow aspect of the grief.

4. It is a transition scene that prepares the audience for the denouement, and it is also a scene that provides closure to the sub-plot of the arranged marriage.

5. The banter of the musicians and Peter is a moment of comic relief which serves to reassure the audience that what is happening is part of the Friar's plan.

LANGUAGE

1. The language of this scene has a poetic and ritualistic aspect to it.

2. The Nurse's dialogue is repetitious and serves the function of a refrain, or is a kind of keening or wailing that emphasises the loss they have experienced. It is as if the Nurse is consoling herself through language.

3. Capulet's speech emphasises the spectre of death as a presence in the play. Death is personified in figurative language and becomes a suitor for Juliet. The language of Capulet is filled, like that of the Nurse, with hyperbole, in an effort to convey his grief and despair.

4. Lady Capulet's language is also filled with repetition. This results in the characters acting almost as a chorus. Their dialogue has a fugue-like effect — it sounds almost like a musical, with its own distinctive counterpoint and harmony.

5. The Friar, when he speaks, is more realistic and controlled. His language focuses on the practical and the moral.

[ACT V]
[SCENE I]

Introduction

Romeo awaits word of Juliet in Mantua, unaware of what is happening. An accident of mistiming and misinformation results in him purchasing poison and preparing to return to Verona.

Enter ROMEO.

Romeo.	If I may trust the flattering truth of sleep	
	My dreams presage some joyful news at hand.	
	My bosom's lord sits lightly in his throne	
	And all this day an unaccustom'd spirit	
	Lifts me above the ground with cheerful thoughts.	5
	I dreamt my lady came and found me dead—	
	Strange dream that gives a dead man leave to think!—	
	And breath'd such life with kisses in my lips	
	That I reviv'd and was an emperor.	
	Ah me, how sweet is love itself possess'd	10
	When but love's shadows are so rich in joy.	

Enter BALTHASAR, *Romeo's man, booted.*

	News from Verona! How, now Balthasar,	
	Dost thou not bring me letters from the Friar?	
	How doth my lady? Is my father well?	
	How doth my Juliet? That I ask again,	15
	For nothing can be ill if she be well.	
Bal.	Then she is well and nothing can be ill.	
	Her body sleeps in Capels' monument,	
	And her immortal part with angels lives.	
	I saw her laid low in her kindred's vault	20
	And presently took post to tell it you.	

Marginal glosses:

1 *truth of sleep* dreams
2 *presage* foretell
3 *bosom's lord* love
11 *love's shadows* dreams of love
21 *took post* started by journey

O pardon me for bringing these ill news,
Since you did leave it for my office, sir.

Romeo.   Is it e'en so? Then I defy you, stars!
Thou know'st my lodging. Get me ink and paper,   25
And hire posthorses. I will hence tonight.

Bal.   I do beseech you sir, have patience.
Your looks are pale and wild and do import
Some misadventure.

Romeo.   Tush, thou art deceiv'd.
Leave me, and do the thing I bid thee do.   30
Hast thou no letters to me from the Friar?

Bal.   No, my good lord.

Romeo.   No matter. Get thee gone.
And hire those horses. I'll be with thee straight.

                        Exit Balthasar.

Well, Juliet, I will lie with thee tonight.
Let's see for means. O mischief thou art swift   35
To enter in the thoughts of desperate men.
I do remember an apothecary—
And hereabouts a dwells—which late I noted
In tatter'd weeds, with overwhelming brows,
Culling of simples. Meagre were his looks,   40
Sharp misery had worn him to the bones,
And in his needy shop a tortoise hung,
An alligator stuff'd, and other skins
Of ill-shap'd fishes; and about his shelves
A beggarly account of empty boxes,   45
Green earthen pots, bladders, and musty seeds,
Remnants of packthread, and old cakes of roses
Were thinly scatter'd to make up a show.
Noting this penury, to myself I said,
'And if a man did need a poison now,   50
Whose sale is present death in Mantua,
Here lives a caitiff wretch would sell it him'.
O, this same thought did but forerun my need,
And this same needy man must sell it me.

---

28 *import*
mean, indicate

37 *apothecary*
drug dealer

40 *Culling*
of simples
Gathering herbs

46 *bladders*
containers

52 *caitiff*
miserable

As I remember, this should be the house.　　　55
Being holiday, the beggar's shop is shut.
What ho! Apothecary!

Enter Apothecary.

Apoth.　　　　　　Who calls so loud?
Romeo.　Come hither, man. I see that thou art poor.
Hold, there is forty ducats. Let me have
A dram of poison, such soon-speeding gear　　60
As will disperse itself through all the veins,
That the life-weary taker may fall dead,
And that the trunk may be discharg'd of breath
As violently as hasty powder fir'd
Doth hurry from the fatal cannon's womb.　　65
Apoth.　Such mortal drugs I have, but Mantua's law
Is death to any he that utters them.
Romeo.　Art thou so bare and full of wretchedness,
And fear'st to die? Famine is in thy cheeks,
Need and oppression starveth in thy eyes,　　70
Contempt and beggary hangs upon thy back.
The world is not thy friend, nor the world's law;
The world affords no law to make thee rich;
Then be not poor, but break it, and take this.
Apoth.　My poverty, but not my will consents.　　75
Romeo.　 I pay thy poverty and not thy will.
Apoth.　 Put this in any liquid thing you will
And drink it off and if you had the strength
Of twenty men it would dispatch you straight.
Romeo.　 There is thy gold—worse poison to men's souls,　80
Doing more murder in this loathsome world
Than these poor compounds that thou mayst not sell.
I sell thee poison, thou hast sold me none.
Farewell, buy food, and get thyself in flesh.
Come, cordial, and not poison, go with me　　85
To Juliet's grave, for there must I use thee.　*Exeunt.*

60 *soon-speeding gear* fatal strong poison

67 *utters them* sells them

85 *cordial* reviving drug

Apothecary.   *Put this in any liquid thing you will*
          And drink it off . . .   *lines 77–8*

SCENE ANALYSIS

ACTION

1. Romeo is on the streets of Mantua. He has had a dream in which he was dead but Juliet came and revived him with kisses, and he became an emperor.
2. Balthasar arrives and tells Romeo that Juliet is dead and lying in the Capulet vault.
3. Romeo curses Fate, 'I defy you stars'. He determines to go to Juliet and take his own life.
4. He goes to a poor apothecary and buys a poison for forty ducats.

THEMES

1. The prologue's description of the lovers as 'star-crossed' is now being fulfilled. Fate is the major theme in the scene. When Romeo says that he will defy the stars, he is challenging Fate and destiny which, for the Elizabethans, would have had ominous resonances.
2. The theme of love also runs throughout the scene with Romeo willing to sacrifice even his life to be with Juliet. In this way, there are echoes of Juliet's own sacrifice in risking death rather than marrying Paris.
3. It is also important to note how Death is becoming Romeo's rival.

CHARACTERISATION

Romeo is initially joyful in this scene. He is awaiting word from Verona and has dreams of Juliet giving him new life. He is obviously very much in love. The news from Verona shocks him and results in him despairing of any future. He is decisive and does not procrastinate. He is clear on the course he must take. He has become a man of action. He displays courage in going to the apothecary, deciding to take poison as a love potion so that he can be with Juliet at any cost.

DRAMATIC EFFECT

1. The scene moves the action of the play forward at great speed. Its brevity reflects the movement toward another climax and emphasises how time overcomes the efforts of the lovers to resist separation. The result is that the rhythm of this section of the play is fast, with the plot moving at a great pace.
2. Romeo's dream has an ironic sense of foreboding. He dreams of being in a vault, with Juliet kissing him and reviving him. This is a reference to Fate.
3. The scene builds suspense. The audience is aware that the Friar's message has not been received and that Romeo is acting on false information. The sense of impending doom and tragedy is palpable.

LANGUAGE

Romeo's description of the apothecary and the language he uses to convince the apothecary to give him poison are filled with images of decay and life's struggles and injustices. His desperation is evident in the cynical tone and pessimistic view of life.

[SCENE II]

Introduction

Friar John tells Friar Lawrence that his message to Romeo was not delivered.
The Friar realises that disaster may be near.

Enter FRIAR JOHN.

Friar J.   Holy Franciscan Friar, Brother, ho!

Enter FRIAR LAURENCE.

Friar L.	This same should be the voice of Friar John.	
	Welcome from Mantua. What says Romeo?	
	Or, if his mind be writ, give me his letter.	
Friar J.	Going to find a barefoot brother out,	5
	One of our order, to associate me,	
	Here in this city visiting the sick,	
	And finding him, the searchers of the town,	
	Suspecting that we both were in a house	
	Where the infectious pestilence did reign,	10
	Seal'd up the doors and would not let us forth,	
	So that my speed to Mantua there was stay'd.	
Friar L.	Who bare my letter then to Romeo?	
Friar J.	I could not send it—here it is again—	
	Nor get a messenger to bring it thee,	15
	So fearful were they of infection.	
Friar L.	Unhappy fortune! By my brotherhood,	
	The letter was not nice but full of charge,	
	Of dear import, and the neglecting it	
	May do much danger. Friar John, go hence,	20
	Get me an iron crow and bring it straight	
	Unto my cell.	
Friar J.	Brother, I'll go and bring it thee.	*Exit.*
Friar L.	Now must I to the monument alone.	
	Within this three hours will fair Juliet wake.	
	She will beshrew me much that Romeo	25
	Hath had no notice of these accidents,	
	But I will write again to Mantua,	
	And keep her at my cell till Romeo come.	
	Poor living corse, clos'd in a dead man's tomb.	*Exit.*

6 *associate me*
accompany me

10 *infectious*
pestilence
plague

21 *crow*
crowbar

SCENE ANALYSIS

ACTION

1. Friar John tells Friar Lawrence that he was unable to deliver his letter to Romeo because he was put in quarantine due to an outbreak of plague.
2. Friar Lawrence realises that Juliet may awaken in the tomb with no-one to release her. He tells John to get him a crow-bar so that he may go to her.

THEMES

The scene focuses on the theme of Fate and how the accidents of destiny can unravel the plans of man.

CHARACTERISATION

The Friar once again is left to devise a course of action that he feels may prevent disaster. His sympathies are with the lovers. He is clear-headed and he acts decisively.

DRAMATIC EFFECT

The audience now wonder whether the Friar can avert disaster and tragedy. Can he get to the vault before Romeo and explain to him what really happened? It is a scene that builds suspense and prepares the audience for the final, climactic moments.

LANGUAGE

The language in this scene is prosaic and colloquial. However, as with the rest of such language, it is actually poetic blank verse which is written in iambic pentameter.

[SCENE III]

Introduction

This scene is eerie and gloomy. Paris and Romeo confront each other in the graveyard before Romeo enters the crypt to see Juliet. Once again, time denies happiness to the lovers and tragedy follows. After the lovers' deaths, their families make peace with each other.

Enter PARIS *and his* Page, *with flowers and sweet water.*

Paris.   Give me thy torch, boy. Hence and stand aloof.

Yet put it out, for I would not be seen.

Under yond yew trees lay thee all along,

Holding thy ear close to the hollow ground;

So shall no foot upon the churchyard tread,   5

Being loose, unfirm, with digging up of graves,

But thou shalt hear it. Whistle then to me

As signal that thou hear'st something approach.

Give me those flowers. Do as I bid thee. Go.

Page.   I am almost afraid to stand alone   10

Here in the churchyard. Yet I will adventure.   *[Retires.]*   11 *adventure*

                              Paris strews the tomb with flowers.   dare to do so

Paris.   Sweet flower, with flowers thy bridal bed I strew.

O woe, thy canopy is dust and stones

Which with sweet water nightly I will dew,

Or wanting that, with tears distill'd by moans.   15

The obsequies that I for thee will keep   16 *obsequies*

Nightly shall be to strew thy grave and weep.   burial rites

                                    Page whistles.

The boy gives warning something doth approach.

What cursed foot wanders this way tonight,

To cross my obsequies and true love's rite?   20

What, with a torch? Muffle me, night, awhile.

                                    [Paris retires.]

Enter ROMEO *and* BALTHASAR *with a torch, a mattock and*

a crow of iron.

Romeo.   Give me that mattock and the wrenching iron.   22 *mattock*

Hold, take this letter. Early in the morning   pickaxe

See thou deliver it to my lord and father.

Give me the light. Upon thy life I charge thee,   25

Whate'er thou hear'st or seest, stand all aloof

And do not interrupt me in my course.   27 *course*

                                     business, work

Why I descend into this bed of death

Is partly to behold my lady's face

But chiefly to take thence from her dead finger   30

A precious ring, a ring that I must use

In dear employment. Therefore hence, be gone.

But if thou jealous dost return to pry

In what I farther shall intend to do,

By heaven I will tear thee joint by joint,   35

And strew this hungry churchyard with thy limbs.

The time and my intents are savage-wild,

More fierce and more inexorable far

Than empty tigers or the roaring sea.

Bal.   I will be gone, sir, and not trouble ye.   40

Romeo.   So shalt thou show me friendship. Take thou that.

Live, and be prosperous, and farewell, good fellow.

Bal.   For all this same, I'll hide me hereabout.

His looks I fear, and his intents I doubt.

                                   [*Balthasar retires.*]

Romeo.   Thou detestable maw, thou womb of death   45

Gorg'd with the dearest morsel of the earth,

Thus I enforce thy rotten jaws to open,

And in despite I'll cram thee with more food.

                              Romeo opens the tomb.

Paris.   This is that banish'd haughty Montague

That murder'd my love's cousin—with which grief   50

It is supposed the fair creature died—

And here is come to do some villainous shame

To the dead bodies. I will apprehend him.

Stop thy unhallow'd toil, vile Montague.

Can vengeance be pursu'd further than death?   55

Condemned villain, I do apprehend thee.

Obey, and go with me, for thou must die.

Romeo.   I must indeed, and therefore came I hither.

Good gentle youth, tempt not a desperate man.

Fly hence and leave me. Think upon these gone.   60

Let them affright thee. I beseech thee, youth,

45 *maw*
stomach

54 *unhallow'd*
toil
wicked work

Put not another sin upon my head

By urging me to fury. O be gone.

By heaven I love thee better than myself,

For I come hither arm'd against myself.   65

Stay not, be gone, live, and hereafter say

A mad man's mercy bid thee run away.

Paris.   I do defy thy conjuration   68 *conjuration*

And apprehend thee for a felon here.   *warning*

Romeo.   Wilt thou provoke me? Then have at thee, boy!   70

They fight.

Page.   O Lord, they fight! I will go call the Watch.

[Exit Page.]

Paris.   O, I am slain! If thou be merciful,

Open the tomb, lay me with Juliet.   *[Paris dies.]*

Romeo.   In faith I will. Let me peruse this face.

Mercutio's kinsman, noble County Paris!   75

What said my man, when my betossed soul   76 *betossed soul*

Did not attend him, as we rode? I think   *confused soul*

He told me Paris should have married Juliet.

Said he not so? Or did I dream it so?

Or am I mad, hearing him talk of Juliet,   80

To think it was so? O, give me thy hand,

One writ with me in sour misfortune's book.

I'll bury thee in a triumphant grave.

A grave? O no, a lantern, slaughter'd youth.

For here lies Juliet, and her beauty makes   85

This vault a feasting presence, full of light.

Death, lie thou there, by a dead man interr'd.   87 *a dead man*

How oft when men are at the point of death   *Romeo*

Have they been merry! Which their keepers call

A lightning before death. O how may I   90

Call this a lightning? O my love, my wife,

Death that hath suck'd the honey of thy breath

Hath had no power yet upon thy beauty.

Thou art not conquer'd. Beauty's ensign yet   94 *ensign*

Is crimson in thy lips and in thy cheeks,   95   *flay*

Romeo.	*. . . Here, here, will I remain*	
	With worms that are thy chambermaids. O here	
	Will I set up my everlasting rest . . .	*line 108–10*

And Death's pale flag is not advanced there.

Tybalt, liest thou there in thy bloody sheet?

O, what more favour can I do to thee

Than with that hand that cut thy youth in twain

To sunder his that was thine enemy?   100

Forgive me, cousin. Ah, dear Juliet,

Why art thou yet so fair? Shall I believe

That unsubstantial Death is amorous,

And that the lean abhorred monster keeps

Thee here in dark to be his paramour?   105   105 *paramour*
                                                        lover

For fear of that I still will stay with thee,

And never from this palace of dim night

Depart again. Here, here, will I remain

With worms that are thy chambermaids. O here

Will I set up my everlasting rest   110

And shake the yoke of inauspicious stars

From this world-wearied flesh. Eyes, look your last.

Arms, take your last embrace! And lips, O you

The doors of breath, seal with a righteous kiss

A dateless bargain to engrossing Death.   115

Come, bitter conduct, come unsavoury guide,

Thou desperate pilot now at once run on

The dashing rocks thy seasick weary bark.

Here's to my love! [*He drinks*.] O true apothecary,

Thy drugs are quick. Thus with a kiss I die.   120

                                    [He] falls.

111 inauspicious stars unlucky stars

117 desperate pilot captain of his own destiny

Enter FRIAR [LAURENCE] *with lantern, crow and spade.*

Friar L. Saint Francis be my speed. How oft tonight

          Have my old feet stumbled at graves. Who's there?

Bal.   Here's one, a friend, and one that knows you well.

Friar L. Bliss be upon you. Tell me, good my friend,

          What torch is yond that vainly lends his light   125

          To grubs and eyeless skulls? As I discern,

          It burneth in the Capels' monument.

Bal.   It doth so, holy sir, and there's my master,

          One that you love.

Friar L.   Who is it?

Bal.   Romeo.

Friar L. How long hath he been there?

Bal.   Full half an hour.   130

Friar L. Go with me to the vault.

Bal.   I dare not, sir.

          My master knows not but I am gone hence,

          And fearfully did menace me with death

          If I did stay to look on his intents.

Friar L. Stay then, I'll go alone. Fear comes upon me.   135

          O, much I fear some ill unthrifty thing.

Bal.   As I did sleep under this yew tree here

I dreamt my master and another fought,
And that my master slew him.

Friar L.   Romeo!

Friar stoops and looks on the blood and weapons.

Alack, alack, what blood is this which stains   140
The stony entrance of this sepulchre?
What mean these masterless and gory swords
To lie discolour'd my this place of peace?
Romeo! O, pale! Who else? What, Paris too?
And steep'd in blood? Ah what an unkind hour   145
Is guilty of this lamentable chance?
The lady stirs.

JULIET *rises.*

Juliet.   O comfortable Friar, where is my lord?
I do remember well where I should be,
And there I am. Where is my Romeo?   150

Friar L. I hear some noise. Lady, come from that nest
Of death, contagion, and unnatural sleep.
A greater power than we can contradict
Hath thwarted our intents. Come, come away.
Thy husband in thy bosom there lies dead,   155
And Paris too. Come, I'll dispose of thee
Among a sisterhood of holy nuns.
Stay not to question, for the Watch is coming.
Come, go, good Juliet. I dare no longer stay.

Juliet.   Go, get thee hence, for I will not away.   160

Exit Friar Laurence.

What's here? A cup clos'd in my true love's hand?
Poison, I see, hath been his timeless end.
O churl. Drunk all, and left no friendly drop
To help me after? I will kiss thy lips.
Haply some poison yet doth hang on them   165
To make me die with a restorative.   [*She kisses him.*]
Thy lips are warm!

141 *sepulchre*
tomb
143 *discolour'd*
abandoned

152 *contagion*
disease

163 *O churl*
fool

Watchman. [*Within.*]   Lead, boy. Which way?

Juliet.   Yea, noise? Then I'll be brief. O happy dagger.

This is thy sheath. There rust, and let me die.

She stabs herself and falls.

Juliet.   *Thy lips are warm!*   *line 167*

Enter Page *and* Watchmen.

Page.   This is the place. There, where the torch doth

burn.   170

1 Watch- The ground is bloody. Search about the
man.   churchyard.

Go, some of you: whoe'er you find, attach.

[*Exeunt some Watchmen.*]

Pitiful sight! Here lies the County slain

And Juliet bleeding, warm, and newly dead,

Who here hath lain this two days buried.   175

Go tell the Prince. Run to the Capulets.

Raise up the Montagues. Some others search.

> *[Exeunt some Watchmen.]*

We see the ground whereon these woes do lie,

But the true ground of all these piteous woes

We cannot without circumstance descry.   180

179 *ground of*
reason for

Enter [several Watchmen *with]* Balthasar.

2 *Watch-* Here's Romeo's man. We found him in the
man.　　　churchyard.

1 *Watch-* Hold him in safety till the Prince come hither.
man.

Enter another Watchman *with* FRIAR LAURENCE.

3 *Watch-* Here is a friar that trembles, sighs and weeps.
man.　　　We took this mattock and this spade from him

As he was coming from this churchyard's side.   185

1 *Watch-* A great suspicion. Stay the friar too.
man.

Enter the PRINCE *[and* Attendants*]*.

Prince.　What misadventure is so early up,

That calls our person from our morning rest?

Enter CAPULET *and* LADY CAPULET *[and* Servants*]*.

Cap.　　What should it be that is so shriek'd abroad?

Lady Cap. O, the people in the street cry 'Romeo',   190

Some 'Juliet', and some 'Paris', and all run

With open outcry toward our monument.

Prince.　What fear is this which startles in our ears?

1 *Watch-* Sovereign, here lies the County Paris slain,
man.

And Romeo dead, and Juliet, dead before,   195

Warm, and new kill'd.

Prince.	Search, seek, and know how this foul murder comes.	
1 Watch-man.	Here is a friar, and slaughter'd Romeo's man, With instruments upon them fit to open	
	These dead men's tombs.	200
Cap.	O heavens! O wife, look how our daughter bleeds!	
	This dagger hath mista'en, for lo, his house	
	Is empty on the back of Montague,	
	And it mis-sheathed in my daughter's bosom.	
Lady Cap.	O me! This sight of death is as a bell	205
	That warns my old age to a sepulchre.	

Enter MONTAGUE [*and* Servants].

Prince.	Come, Montague, for thou art early up	
	To see thy son and heir now early down.	
Mont.	Alas, my liege, my wife is dead tonight.	
	Grief of my son's exile hath stopp'd her breath.	210
	What further woe conspires against mine age?	
Prince.	Look, and thou shalt see.	
Mont.	O thou untaught! What manners is in this,	
	To press before thy father to a grave?	
Prince.	Seal up the mouth of outrage for a while	215
	Till we can clear these ambiguities	
	And know their spring, their head, their true descent,	
	And then will I be general of your woes	
	And lead you, even to death. Meantime forbear,	
	And let mischance be slave to patience.	220
	Bring forth the parties of suspicion.	
Friar L.	I am the greatest, able to do least,	
	Yet most suspected, as the time and place	
	Doth make against me, of this direful murder.	
	And here I stand, both to impeach and purge	225
	Myself condemned and myself excus'd.	
Prince.	Then say at once what thou dost know in this.	
Friar L.	I will be brief, for my short date of breath	
	Is not so long as is a tedious tale.	

213 *untaught*
ignorant person

220 *mischance be*
slave to patience
disaster be ruled
by patience

225 *impeach*
accuse

Romeo, there dead, was husband to that Juliet,   230
And she, there dead, that Romeo's faithful wife.
I married them, and their stol'n marriage day
Was Tybalt's doomsday, whose untimely death
Banish'd the new-made bridegroom from this city;
For whom, and not for Tybalt, Juliet pin'd.   235
You, to remove that siege of grief from her,
Betroth'd and would have married her perforce
To County Paris. Then comes she to me
And with wild looks bid me devise some mean
To rid her from this second marriage,   240
Or in my cell there would she kill herself.
Then gave I her—so tutor'd by my art—
A sleeping potion, which so took effect
As I intended, for it wrought on her
The form of death. Meantime I writ to Romeo   245
That he should hither come as this dire night
To help to take her from her borrow'd grave,
Being the time the potion's force should cease.
But he which bore my letter, Friar John,
Was stay'd by accident, and yesternight   250
Return'd my letter back. Then all alone
At the prefixed hour of her waking
Came I to take her from her kindred's vault,
Meaning to keep her closely at my cell
Till I conveniently could send to Romeo.   255
But when I came, some minute ere the time
Of her awakening, here untimely lay
The noble Paris and true Romeo dead.
She wakes; and I entreated her come forth
And bear this work of heaven with patience,   260
But then a noise did scare me from the tomb
And she, too desperate, would not go with me
But, as it seems, did violence on herself.
All this I know; and to the marriage
Her Nurse is privy; and if aught in this   265

237 *perforce*
by force
239 *mean*
method, plan

245 *form*
appearance

Miscarried by my fault, let my old life   *265 privy*
Be sacrific'd some hour before his time   aware
Unto the rigour of severest law.

Prince. We still have known thee for a holy man.
Where's Romeo's man? What can he say to this?   270

Bal. I brought my master news of Juliet's death,
And then in post he came from Mantua
To this same place, to this same monument.
This letter he early bid me give his father
And threaten'd me with death, going in the vault,   275
If I departed not and left him there.

Prince. Give me the letter, I will look on it.
Where is the County's Page that rais'd the Watch?
Sirrah, what made your master in this place?

Page. He came with flowers to strew his lady's grave   280
And bid me stand aloof, and so I did.
Anon comes one with light to ope the tomb
And by and by my master drew on him,
And then I ran away to call the Watch.

285 make good
confirm

Montague.   *There shall no figure at such rate be set*
              As that of true and faithful Juliet.   *lines 300–301*

Prince.	This letter doth make good the Friar's words:	285
	Their course of love, the tidings of her death,	
	And here he writes that he did buy a poison	
	Of a poor pothecary, and therewithal	
	Came to this vault to die and lie with Juliet.	
	Where be these enemies? Capulet, Montague,	290
	See what a scourge is laid upon your hate,	
	That heaven finds means to kill your joys with love;	
	And I, for winking at your discords too,	
	Have lost a brace of kinsmen. All are punish'd.	
Cap.	O brother Montague, give me thy hand.	295
	This is my daughter's jointure, for no more	
	Can I demand.	
Mont.	But I can give thee more,	
	For I will raise her statue in pure gold,	
	That whiles Verona by that name is known,	
	There shall no figure at such rate be set	300
	As that of true and faithful Juliet.	
Cap.	As rich shall Romeo's by his lady's lie,	
	Poor sacrifices of our enmity.	
Prince.	A glooming peace this morning with it brings:	
	The sun for sorrow will not show his head.	305
	Go hence to have more talk of these sad things.	
	Some shall be pardon'd, and some punished,	
	For never was a story of more woe	
	Than this of Juliet and her Romeo. *Exeunt.*	

293 *winking at*
closing my eyes

discords
disagreement

296 *jointure*
the portion the
bridegroom
brings to the
bride

300 *at such rate*
high value

304 *glooming*
dark and
depressing

Scene Analysis

ACTION

1. Paris has come to the crypt to put flowers on Juliet's tomb. He tells his boy to keep watch and to whistle when anyone approaches.

2. Romeo and Balthasar arrive. Romeo tells his boy that he wishes to see his bride's

face again and to retrieve a precious ring. He instructs him to leave and not to return, under pain of death.

3. Romeo opens the tomb, is recognised by Paris who confronts and challenges him.
4. Romeo fights and kills Paris and then drags his body into the tomb.
5. He lays Paris's body next to Juliet, who seems untouched by death.
6. Romeo embraces Juliet, kisses her for a last time, takes the potion and dies.
7. The Friar arrives and is shocked to hear that Romeo has been there for half an hour. He enters the tomb and finds the bodies of Paris and Romeo.
8. Juliet awakens. The Friar tells her the shocking news and urges her to come away, saying he will place her in a convent.
9. Juliet refuses and the Friar leaves in fear, knowing the Watch is coming.
10. Juliet, finding no poison left, tries to get some in a kiss from her husband's lips, but to no avail. With the Watch approaching, she takes Romeo's dagger and kills herself.
11. The Watchman apprehends Balthasar, Paris's page and the Friar, and sends for Prince Escalus, the Capulets and the Montagues.
12. The Friar explains all to the Prince and it is confirmed by a letter written to Montague by Romeo.
13. The Prince lays the blame on the Montague and Capulet feud. He exonerates the Friar and Balthasar.
14. The families are reconciled and the fathers promise to erect golden statues in memory of their dead children.

THEMES

1. The tragedy is caused, as Prince Escalus says, by the 'enmity' that has existed between the families. The futility of the feud is all too apparent in this scene.
2. Love is presented as a powerful force. The deaths of the lovers are not in vain; their love eventually unites the community. The statues when erected will be symbols of the power of their love.
3. Although the deaths of the lovers are tragic, in some ways they may also be regarded as a victory. In death they are united, they escape the world of the feud and overcome Fate. They also transcend time, so that Romeo and Juliet will always exist in memory as passionate young lovers whose love for each other will never diminish.

CHARACTERISATION

1. Romeo emerges as an heroic figure in this scene. He fears nothing and confronts death in his efforts to be reunited with Juliet. There is no hesitation in his actions

as they are guided by love. His killing of Paris is unavoidable and he honours his promise to the young noble by laying his body beside that of Juliet.

2. Juliet shows a firmness when encouraged by the Friar to leave the tomb. She refuses to desert Romeo and displays great love and loyalty in her unflinching decisiveness.

3. Paris is the conventional courtly lover in this scene. He has come to the tomb to place flowers and to weep, more out of a duty as Juliet's former fiancé than out of romantic love. He is a young nobleman who wishes to act in a mannerly fashion, doing what is right. He feels obliged to challenge Romeo out of loyalty to Juliet and to the Capulet family. Despite his bravery and nobility his death is a tragic waste which occurs out of ignorance of the reality of events.

4. Friar Lawrence emerges as an unfortunate figure in this scene. Despite his best efforts, he cannot change the course of Fate. His fear causes him to abandon Juliet in the tomb. The love of the hero and heroine and the dreadful pattern of events horrify and shock him. His desertion of her when she most needs companionship recalls the Nurse's desertion of her earlier in the play.

5. The parents of the lovers are grief-stricken at what has happened. Romeo's mother has already died of a broken heart because of his banishment and now his father, mourning his wife, has to contend with the death of his son. Lady Capulet is shocked by what she sees and the realisation of what has happened chastens her. Her husband, Capulet, is the first to offer peace and to reconcile himself with his enemy, providing a resolution to the play. Capulet realises his mistakes and is eager to let the example of their children guide them in the future.

6. The Prince, as ever, shows himself to be a wise ruler. He blames the deaths on the feud, but he also takes responsibility himself for what has happened. He maintains that if he had been harsher with Capulet and Montague, things would not have got to this state.

DRAMATIC EFFECT

1. The churchyard, tomb and the night-time setting all contribute to establishing a mood of fear and doom. It is a terrifying setting. The Page is afraid of being alone and the Friar, when he arrives, only remains a short time before running away.

2. There is a lot of tension and suspense in the scene. The audience wonders whether the Friar will arrive in time to save Romeo and help Juliet. The audience is horrified at the confrontation between Romeo and Paris, realising that Paris, who is acting in a noble manner, could possibly kill Romeo or be killed himself.

3. The descent to the tomb, with Romeo viewing the body of his dead wife, is filled with pathos and her discovery of him dead beside her is heart wrenching.

4. The scene builds to a climax that involves a lot of movement and confusion before bringing about the reconciliation of the families.

LANGUAGE

1. Romeo's language is passionate and delivered in blank verse. It is filled with violent images and has an energy to it that reflects his violent disposition.
2. Paris, on the other hand, initially speaks in verse, indicating how conventional his behaviour is. He is present as a contrast to Romeo and reminds us of how much Romeo has changed and grown since the opening scene when his thoughts on love were delivered in puns, oxymoron and clichés.
3. Romeo addresses Death as a rival. He personifies Death and seeks to defeat him in competition for Juliet.
4. The Prince speaks eloquently and directly. His language is literal until the final speech when, in an effort to convey the depth of the tragedy, it becomes figurative.

Assessing Character

INTRODUCTION

The novelist Jane Austen distinguished between two kinds of characters: complex and shallow. For her, complex characters were those who were affected by experience, who changed or developed because of what happened. Shallow characters, on the other hand, were those whose lives seemed untouched by experience, who seemed to have no inner life and who did not change despite what happened to them.

In drama, one can distinguish between characters who tend to be one-dimensional, i.e. who seem to lack depth of feeling and who never really develop, and those who are fully rounded, almost three-dimensional.

ONE-DIMENSIONAL

In Romeo and Juliet, for example, Tybalt can be regarded as a one-dimensional character. He has no real range of emotions and appears incapable of development. When he first appears in the play, his intention is to cause confrontation and conflict. This does not change as the play progresses. At the Capulet feast he sends for his rapier and wants to punish Romeo for coming

> . . . in spite
> To scorn at our solemnity this night.

Even when his uncle Capulet requests that Tybalt

> . . . be patient, take no note of him.
> It is my will, the which if thou respect,
> Show a fair presence and put off these frowns,

Tybalt rants 'I'll not endure him'. He is unable to control his temper, resulting in Capulet referring to him as 'a saucy boy' and 'a princox'.

The next time we hear of Tybalt is when Mercutio and Benvolio discuss the challenge he is said to have delivered to Romeo. Following this, his final entrance is in the fight scene where, once again, he insists on confrontation.

Although the Nurse refers to Tybalt as —

> Tybalt, the best friend I had!
> O courteous Tybalt! Honest gentleman

and Juliet calls him 'my dearest cousin', the audience never see this side of his character. The Tybalt presented to us is a character whose role appears to be one of dramatic and symbolic intent. Tybalt, in effect, personifies the feud and his presence in a scene introduces tension and suspense, always moving the action towards the possibility of climax. In this way he may be regarded as one-dimensional, because we never see the full human being, but only that part of him that is vital to the plot. Consequently, he does not develop or change in the course of the drama.

TWO-DIMENSIONAL

The Nurse is also someone who is not really affected by the action that occurs, although her character is much more rounded and complex than that of Tybalt.

In many ways, in the course of the play, it is not the Nurse who changes but the audience's perception of her.

At the beginning of the play the Nurse is garrulous and comical. She is an earthy woman with a vulgar and bawdy humour. We recognise her as being close to Juliet and someone who seems to love the heroine.

However, in acting as a go-between for the lovers, she is essentially betraying her employers, the Capulet parents. She is, after all, helping their thirteen-year-old daughter to have a relationship with the teenage son of their enemy. Yet, we tend to ignore or forget this aspect of her behaviour because she acts in the interests of the lovers. We enjoy her zest for life:

> Go, girl, seek happy nights to happy days

her ironic humour:

> I am the drudge and toil in your delight;
> But you shall bear the burden soon at night

and we enjoy the intimacy of her scenes with the young girl when she teases her about her messages to Romeo, feigning tiredness and age. Yet, she eventually betrays Juliet. When the heroine most needs her,

> O God, O Nurse, how shall this be prevented? . . .
> Comfort me, counsel me . . .
> What say'st thou? Hast thou not a word of joy?
> Some comfort, Nurse.

she disappoints and reveals her fickle nature, leading Juliet to say of her:

> . . . O most wicked fiend!
> Is it more sin to wish me thus forsworn,
> Or to dispraise my lord with that same tongue
> Which she hath praised him with above compare
> So many thousand times? Go, counsellor!
> Thou and my bosom henceforth shall be twain.

This reversal of how the Nurse is perceived is a shock. Because of our allegiance to the heroine we change our own view of the Nurse and realise just how shallow a character she is. Essentially, then, it is not the Nurse who changes significantly in the course of the play, but our perception of her.

COMPLEX: THREE-DIMENSIONAL

Both Romeo and Juliet are fully realised characters in the play. Each is transformed by what happens and the audience witness all aspects of their natures.

ROMEO

At the start of the play Romeo is a well-regarded young man, a courtly gentleman. His comments about his love for Rosaline are delivered in a self-conscious and ornate prose which is punctuated by hyperbole, paradox and oxymoron.

> Love is a smoke made with the fume of sighs;
> Being purg'd, a fire sparkling in lovers' eyes;
> Being vexed, a sea nourish'd with lovers' tears;
> What is it else? A madness most discreet,
> A choking gall, and a preserving sweet.

His speech is intellectual rather than emotional, and betrays him as a young man of fashion.

When he initially talks to Juliet at the Capulet feast, their conversation is conventional and playful, taking the form of a sonnet (until their first kiss). But then Juliet wittily remarks to him that 'You kiss by th' book', a gentle put-down that suggests that his kiss is more mannered than sincere.

However, Juliet changes him. He becomes obsessed with her rather than merely with the notion of love. He no longer confuses a fascination with the idea of love with the reality of being in love with another person:

> Amen, amen, but come what sorrow can,
> It cannot countervail the exchange of joy
> That one short minute gives me in her sight.

His speech moves from rhyme to blank verse, which indicates a more passionate and sincere form of expression.

> The time and my intents are savage wild
> More fierce and more inexorable far
> Than empty tigers or the roaring sea.

By the end of the play his language stands in direct contrast to the more formal and self-conscious expression of Paris:

> Sweet flower, with flowers thy bridal bed I strew.
> O woe! Thy canopy is dust and stones
> Which with sweet water nightly I will dew,
> Or, wanting that, with tears distill'd by moans.

On a much more obvious level, you should note that Paris arrives at the crypt with flowers to mourn Juliet, while Romeo arrives with 'that mattock and the wrenching iron' with the intention of tearing the crypt open.

JULIET

Juliet also changes from an obedient and dutiful daughter who initially says about Paris to her mother that:

> I'll look to like, if looking liking move,
> But no more deep will I endart mine eye
> Than your consent gives strength to make it fly.

However, all this changes once she has fallen in love with Romeo, when she says:

> My bounty is as boundless as the sea,
> My love as deep: the more I give to thee
> The more I have, for both are infinite.

In her declarations of love, she makes her decisions independently of anyone:

> And all my fortunes at thy foot I'll lay
> And follow thee my lord throughout the world.

Their clandestine relationship exists outside the bounds of conventional ties and duties, so when Juliet hears that her father has arranged her marriage to Paris, she can no longer obey him:

> Now by Saint Peter's Church, and Peter too,
> He shall not make me there a joyful bride.
> I wonder at this haste, that I must wed
> Ere he that should be husband comes to woo.

Her father's reaction, not knowing of her marriage to the banished Romeo, is to interpret her refusal as disobedience and ungratefulness:

> Hang thee young baggage, disobedient wretch!
> I tell thee what — get thee to church on Thursday
> Or never after look me in the face.

It is the complexity of these relationships and the effect of experience on the lives of the characters that make them fully rounded individuals who engage the interest and concern of the audience. While a character such as Tybalt may interest the audience because of the tension he brings to scenes, and while the Nurse may amuse us with her mannerisms and comical remarks, neither of them ever elicits the sympathy and concern of the audience in the way that the central characters do. We do not mourn the death of Tybalt, we do not miss the Nurse when she retires from the action; they exist only in terms of their function regarding the central characters.

AUDIENCE'S PERCEPTION OF CHARACTER

The way an audience relates to a character is largely determined by three things: reputation, dialogue and behaviour.

REPUTATION

How other characters relate to an individual affects our view of that person. We are also influenced by what the other characters say about a character, what they say to the character and how they talk to the character. For example, when Romeo attends the Capulet feast, Capulet himself says of the young man that:

> A bears him like a portly gentleman;
> And, to say truth, Verona brags of him
> To be a virtuous and well-governed youth.

On the other hand, Mercutio says of Tybalt that he is

> . . . the very butcher of a silk button — a
> duellist, a duellist, a gentleman of the very first
> house, of the first and second cause.

DIALOGUE

What a character actually says betrays the kind of person he or she is. Dialogue indicates the character's moods, how he or she regards other characters, and whether he or she is mercenary or considerate. Essentially the manner of speaking and the tone of what is said suggest the kinds of relationship the character has with others in the play. For example, after the death of Tybalt, Juliet defends Romeo saying:

> Upon his brow shame is asham'd to sit,
> For 'tis a throne where honour may be crown'd,
> Sole monarch of the universal earth.
> O, what a beast was I to chide at him.

These remarks indicate the depth of her feelings for her husband. With these lines Juliet reiterates her love for her husband and suggests to the Nurse that he is not to be criticised.

BEHAVIOUR

The actions of a character — what the person does, how he/she behaves — is crucial to our determining whether the character is sincere or not. One thing that affects our view of the person is whether he or she is motivated by selfishness or by consideration for the well-being of others. We are also influenced by whether a character's actions are courageous, cowardly, or foolhardy.

Planning and Writing Answers on Characters

❧

QUESTIONS REQUIRING YOU TO FOCUS ON ONE CHARACTER

1. Choose about seven or eight good adjectives that you think provide an accurate portrait of the person.
2. Arrange the adjectives in pairs that either have a common theme or are in opposition.
3. Think of at least one incident for each set of adjectives that best illustrates these qualities of character.
4. Arrange the scenes you have chosen in chronological order so that your answer will have a logical development with a proper beginning, middle and end. Or arrange the adjectives in such a way that their order indicates a change in the character during the course of the play (a character, for example, may move from being cowardly to being brave).

EXAMPLES OF ADJECTIVES

Examples of adjectives that could be used to describe characters include:

The Nurse: pompous, amoral, garrulous, comical, fickle, lusty, pragmatic, bawdy, insensitive.

Tybalt: vain, arrogant, petulant, sardonic, one-dimensional, fearless, villainous, feared.

Juliet: dutiful, sincere, imaginative, enchanting, impulsive, passionate, courageous, wilful, independent, innocent, beautiful, witty.

Romeo: courtly, impetuous, respected, popular, moral, melancholic, loyal, honourable, courageous, fearless, charming, witty.

HOW TO STRUCTURE ANSWERS

THE OPENING PARAGRAPH

The opening paragraph of your answer should provide a context for the overall

163

answer. It should introduce its concerns — the topic you intend to cover — and should suggest the direction the answer will take. More than anything, the answer must address the question and indicate that it will focus on the issues you have been asked to discuss.

Sample Question

With reference to a play you have studied focus on one character from the play and discuss how that character changes as a result of events in the play.

Sample Opening Paragraphs

1. The life of Juliet of Capulet, the teenage heroine of Shakespeare's *Romeo and Juliet*, is destroyed by a feud between members of her family and those of the Montague household. She secretly marries Romeo of Montague, but their love for each other is unable to escape the fierce feud waged by their families.

2. Romeo of Montague, the hero of Shakespeare's *Romeo and Juliet*, changes from being a reserved and charming youth to a passionate and impetuous lover in the course of the play. It is his love for Juliet of Capulet, the daughter of his father's enemy, which transforms him. Caught up in a feud waged by their families, the two most powerful in Verona, the lovers unsuccessfully attempt to invent a world of their own.

CENTRAL PARAGRAPHS

Remember that the central paragraphs of your answer should not be a mere summary of the play's action. You must comment on the action and the characters, indicating your opinion and interpretation, giving good reasons for your views. Your views must be properly supported by relevant quotation or reference.

Sample Question

Let us imagine that you have been asked to 'Outline the influence of a character on events in your play, illustrating that character's importance to the plot.'

Approaching the Writing

To compose a standard central paragraph about a character:
• Comment immediately on the person, using one or two of your adjectives.

Example: The Nurse is a garrulous person.

- Illustrate what you mean by reference to the action of a particular scene, indicating just what happens and demonstrating your knowledge of the plot by using quotations.

Example: When Lady Capulet first discusses the prospect of marriage to Paris with Juliet, the Nurse keeps interrupting with a vulgar anecdote about Juliet falling when she was a baby:

> 'Yea,' quoth my husband, 'fall'st upon thy face?
> Thou wilt fall backward when thou comest to age.'

- Comment directly on the behaviour of the character in the scene. Consider whether his or her actions are selfish or considerate, or comment on how the character relates to others in the scene.

Example: This incident illustrates the Nurse's long service with the family and her closeness to Juliet. However, it also reveals her to be a common person. Although Lady Capulet tries to restrain the Nurse:

> Enough of this, I pray thee, hold thy peace

the Nurse persists, laughing heartily and retelling the story a number of times.

- An option in your discussion is to examine the use of themes in the scene with reference to the characters. However, this is an option and you may not have time to include it or you may find that it is not always relevant to every aspect of your discussion.

Example: Essentially, her bawdy memory reveals her view of love to be limited to the physical, while the scene itself indicates that Lady Capulet's attitude to love tends to be contractual.

How the Full Paragraph Looks

The Nurse is a garrulous person. When Lady Capulet first discusses the prospect of marriage to Paris with Juliet, the Nurse keeps interrupting with a vulgar anecdote about Juliet falling when she was a baby:

> 'Yea,' quoth my husband, 'fall'st upon thy face?
> Thou wilt fall backward when thou comest to age.'

This incident illustrates the Nurse's long service with the family and her closeness to Juliet. However, it also reveals her to be a common person. Although Lady Capulet tries to restrain the Nurse:

> Enough of this, I pray thee, hold thy peace

she persists, laughing heartily and retelling the story a number of times.

Essentially, her bawdy memory reveals her view of love to be limited to the physical, while the scene itself indicates that Lady Capulet's attitude to love tends to be contractual. However, initially the Nurse seems comical and her bawdy humour provides the audience with plenty of entertainment.

COMPARE AND CONTRAST

Some questions require you to compare and/or contrast two characters. Questions that use the term 'compare' tend to be open in how you can approach them. However, while 'compare' suggests looking for similarities, the term 'contrast' has to do with looking at differences. So, a question that uses both words requires you to discuss two characters in terms of how they are alike and dissimilar.

EXAMPLE

Decide upon two characters you feel could be compared successfully. For example: the Nurse and Mercutio; the Nurse and Friar Lawrence; Mercutio and Tybalt; Capulet parents and Montague parents; Romeo and Juliet. Again, you must have about seven or eight good adjectives around which to build your answer.

The characters should not be written about independently of each other: there is no point in writing about one character for a page and then writing about the second character for another page, as if it were two separate essays — that is not comparison!

Ideally, you should write about both characters in each paragraph. If you are unable to do this, then each character should be written about in alternate paragraphs.

Best Method

1. Think of a series of headings, about four, that will act as paragraph themes.
2. Compare the characters using these headings as guidelines.
3. Each heading should result in one paragraph.

4. Each paragraph should focus on one or possibly two incidents, which will act as a reference or illustration to support your discussion.
5. Give your answer a chronology: beginning/middle/end.
6. Trace the development of the characters in some kind of order.
7. Connect your paragraphs.

The following two paragraphs focus on two characters, the Nurse and Mercutio, under the heading of 'Humour'. The answer is part of a question that requires a student to 'Take two characters from a play studied by you, and compare and contrast them, illustrating their influence on the action of the play.'

Example

The Nurse and Mercutio both give the play a comic dimension. However, their humour is different. His jokes are clever witticisms that make great use of puns. Bantering with Romeo, he says:

> Sure wit, follow me this jest now, till thou hast
> worn out thy pump, that when the single soul of it is
> worn,the jest may remain after the wearing solely
> singular.

His wit is often also sardonic, mocking the vanities and follies of those around him. He ridicules the Nurse's pomposity with —

> Good Peter, to hide her face; for her fan's the
> fairer face . . .

while he sneers at Tybalt's reputation, saying:

> More, than prince of cats, I can tell you. O! He is
> the courageous captain of compliments.

Mercutio's humour reveals him as a sophisticated and imaginative young person. The Nurse's humour, on the other hand, is baser, more crude, tending, at times, towards the farcical. When she is jeered, she returns with:

> And a speak anything against me I'll take him
> down, and a were lustier than he is, and twenty such
> Jacks.

She also has great fun teasing Juliet by delaying the messages from Romeo with references to her health and tiredness:

> Lord, how my head aches! What a head have I:
> It beats as it would fall in twenty pieces.
> My back o' t'other side — ah, my back, my back!

The Nurse's comic character, in scenes such as these, gives the play a very realistic and human dimension. Her gossipy nature and no-nonsense attitude provides the tragedy with a domestic aspect.

Planning and Writing Answers on a Scene

WHAT TO LOOK FOR

The scenes of a drama contain many different features and it is important to identify and distinguish these features before attempting to write about a scene.

FOUR MAJOR AREAS TO CONSIDER

1. INCIDENT

A scene's action should attempt to reveal certain qualities in a character — what happens in a scene should, as Henry James once said, be an 'illustration of character'. Therefore, any real understanding of what is occurring in a scene involves being able to summarise, i.e. to provide a synopsis of the events. Before discussing a scene make a list of the things that happen in it.

For example, Act I Scene V

1. The Capulet house is prepared for a party and for dancing.
2. Capulet welcomes his guests and urges them to dance, telling his cousin that they are both past their dancing days.
3. Romeo sees Juliet dancing with Paris and is smitten.
4. Tybalt recognises Romeo and sends for his sword.
5. Capulet dismisses Tybalt, who vows vengeance.
6. Romeo approaches Juliet and kisses her.
7. The Nurse tells Romeo that Juliet is a Capulet.
8. The Nurse tells Juliet that Romeo is a Montague.

2. CHARACTER

How a character behaves and relates to other people, what he says and how he says it, suggest attitudes and indicate certain moral qualities. Part of what you should attempt to do is consider whether the actions of a character are selfish or considerate, whether her actions are disruptive or likely to offend, and whether the character cares about how others are affected by her behaviour.

For example, Act III Scene I

1. Mercutio's behaviour is reckless and arrogant. He refuses to leave the square despite Benvolio's warnings to do so. He confronts Tybalt and almost looks for offence. On the one hand his speech is sardonic and comical, but it is also haughty and dismissive.

2. Tybalt is threatening and belligerent. He has only one aim — to avenge the insult he thinks Romeo has given by attending the Capulet feast. Tybalt is scornful of everyone else. He rejects Romeo's efforts to avoid conflict and is intent on confrontation. His actions, like those of Mercutio, are anarchic, with no regard for the Prince's warning and with no concern for how his actions will affect others around him.

3. Romeo is aware that he now has obligations to Tybalt as he is married to Tybalt's cousin. He attempts to placate Tybalt, even taking his insults, willing to be publicly ridiculed rather than be disloyal to Juliet. His eventual fight with Tybalt is provoked by passionate grief and is the result of loyalty to his dead friend, Mercutio, for whose death he feels responsible. Romeo, then, unlike the other two characters, is a victim of circumstance and of Fate.

3. DRAMATIC IMPACT

Consider the effect of the action on the audience. What mood is established by the events? What is the setting for the scene? Can you discern the rhythm of the scene? What elements of *conflict*, *tension* and *suspense* are present? Does the scene build to a *climax*? Think about the scene in terms of its *performance* on stage.

For example, Act I Scene I

1. The scene is filled with a youthful energy. It is tremendously colourful. There is a lot of movement. The rhythm is fast and vibrant. The feud engages the audience and establishes the basic context for the play's action.

2. The mood is initially comical. The tone of the Capulets and Montagues is one of mockery and disdain. Then the brawl causes the mood to become tense and dangerous. Finally, a more subdued mood pervades when the melancholic Romeo confesses his unrequited love for Rosaline to Benvolio. The function of this is to develop the action, but also to contrast Romeo's love with the hatred of the two families.

3. An atmosphere of tension dominates the scene. The families are in conflict. The Prince issues an ultimatum. Throughout the scene there is suspense as the audience wait for characters to be injured or killed in the brawl that, with Tybalt's appearance, seems to be beyond control and envelops young and old.

For example, Act IV Scene III

1. The mood is one of despair and desolation. Having bid goodnight to her Mother and the Nurse, Juliet must now take the potion given to her by the Friar. She is completely isolated and obviously very nervous and uncertain, longing for companionship, but unable to confide in anyone.

2. The scene has great suspense. The audience is concerned for Juliet, but helpless — the world of the stage and the theatregoer being very separate and yet inseparable. The audience can only watch, and this frustrates and fascinates them — they cannot advise or warn Juliet.

3. Juliet outlines the dangers she faces — treachery, suffocation, madness — which adds to the tension, gripping the attention of the audience and eliciting their sympathy. The scene has an intimacy to it that contrasts with the confrontation of previous scenes. The setting is a bedroom which increases the sense of secrecy and intimacy. It reaches a horrifying climax in Juliet drinking the potion.

4. THEMES

The action of a scene and the interplay of characters usually develops some of the play's central themes. It is important, therefore, to ask: (a) how a scene helps develop plot; (b) what it reveals about character; and (c) what themes are involved.

For example, Act I Scene I

1. The theme of hatred is evident in the feud.
2. The theme of love is dramatised in Romeo's conversation with Benvolio.
3. Themes of youth and age are present in the way characters from every generation become involved in the brawl.
4. The theme of time is evident in the ongoing nature of the feud.
5. The theme of the relationship between parents and children is evident in the Montagues' concern for the whereabouts of their son.

PLANNING THE WRITING

Let us say that you have been asked to 'Take a particular scene from a play you have studied which you feel conveyed the themes of the play. Outline the action of the scene and illustrate what aspects of the play's themes were highlighted in the scene.'

1. DEVELOPMENT

Divide the scene into sections — chart its beginning, middle and end.

For example, Act III Scene V

1. The lovers part after their wedding night.
2. Lady Capulet tells Juliet of her plans to poison Romeo.
3. Juliet's mother tells her of the proposed marriage to Paris on Thursday.
4. Juliet's father is furious to hear of her refusal to marry and threatens her with disinheritance.
5. The Nurse is no help to Juliet and Juliet feels betrayed.

2. THE QUESTION

Focus on what the question asks you to discuss. Is the question concerned with the scene's portrayal of character? Does it ask how a scene dramatises themes? Or does the question focus on staging or dramatic impact?

3. PERSONAL RESPONSE

Remember that the answer should convey how you feel about the play. An answer must involve an element of personal response.

4. SYNOPSIS AND CRITICISM

It is not enough merely to summarise the action of a scene when you are answering a question or to tell the story of what happens in your own words. Questions require you to demonstrate that you understand what happens, that you are capable of critical analysis and that you have opinions. The answer, therefore, has to be a blend of brief summary (in the form of references or quotes) and criticism.

5. QUOTATIONS

1. You must have a knowledge of important lines from the play. It displays an interest in the work and indicates that you are well prepared.
2. Quotations should be used carefully to support your opinion and to strengthen your argument.
3. Keep quotations reasonably short. There is no real point in writing out a fifteen-line speech just to show that you learned it: quotations are used to back up your view, not to replace your view. Your answer should be sprinkled with quotations relevant to what you are discussing.

ANSWER FORMAT

Opening Paragraphs

An opening paragraph is really an introduction to your discussion. It is important to control it well and not to let it ramble. Let your opening paragraph be quite short. Aim to let it provide a context for your discussion.

The opening of an answer should:
1. State the title of the play.
2. Give the name of the author.
3. Address the question being asked, using the key word or term.
4. Very briefly outline the action of the scene.

Examples

Sample Question

Taking any scene from your play that you thought held the audience's attention well, discuss the dramatic impact of the scene and outline why you considered the scene successful. You must give the name of the play and author, and support your answer with relevant references or quotations.

Sample Introduction 1

The Capulet feast (Act I Scene V) in Shakespeare's tragedy *Romeo and Juliet* is a scene containing colour, contrast and suspense. This is the scene in which the teenagers, Romeo and Juliet, from the feuding families of Montague and Capulet, meet for the first time and fall in love. It is a scene that dramatises the play's opposing themes of love and hate, age and youth, with great dramatic tension.

Sample Introduction 2

The fight scene (Act III Scene I) in Shakespeare's tragedy *Romeo and Juliet* is a turning point in the play, filled with conflict and suspense and having great dramatic impact. In this scene, Tybalt of Capulet kills Mercutio, a kinsman of the Prince and Romeo of Montague's close friend, an act that provokes Romeo to avenge Mercutio's death, although it means disaster for him.

Sample Introduction 3

The opening scene (Act I Scene I) in Shakespeare's tragedy *Romeo and Juliet* provides an exciting and vibrant start to this play about young love and hatred. In this scene, the feud between Verona's most powerful families, Montague and

Capulet, erupts on the city's streets, disturbing the peace and endangering citizens. It is a scene filled with comedy and danger which immediately captures the audience's attention.

CENTRAL PARAGRAPHS

The central paragraphs of your answer are really where you dissect a scene, give your opinions, indicate just how you interpret the action and try to convey what you experienced. It is important to work through the scene in a logical way and to develop an argument, or to build up some overall picture of what went on.

In a central paragraph you should:
1. Briefly outline some incident that occurs.
2. Use quotes when describing what happens.
3. Discuss the action, commenting on —
    (a) what it reveals about character *or*
    (b) the themes that are involved *or*
    (c) the use of language or imagery *or*
    (d) the building of tension or suspense.
4. Try to include some aspect of personal response.
5. Relate your discussion to the terms of the question.

For example, discussing Act IV Scene III

Paragraph 2 of an Answer

Juliet is initially afraid of being left alone: 'I'll call them back again to comfort me.' Her future is uncertain and she is obviously nervous of taking the potion that the Friar has given her:

> . . . God knows when we shall meet again.
> I have a faint cold fear thrills through my veins
> That almost freezes up the heat of life.

Her expression of her fears engages the audience and elicits its sympathy for her plight. It is almost as if Juliet is looking for reassurance or assistance in the task that she is to perform.

I feel it is a moment that emphasises her vulnerability. For me, her anxiety is obvious in her desire to 'call them back again to comfort me', even though she realises that she must face her fate alone: 'Nurse! — What should she do here?'

For example, discussing Act V Scene III

Third Paragraph of an Answer

When Paris confronts Romeo, he does so out of duty rather than passion:

> Condemned villain, I do apprehend thee.
> Obey, and go with me, for thou must die.

The distraught Romeo initially shows restraint and warns Paris:

> Put not another sin upon my head
> By urging me to fury. O be gone!

However, Paris disregards the warning and is killed. A contrast is obviously intended when the incident brings Juliet's husband and her suitor face to face. The courtly Paris highlights how much Romeo has changed. Romeo's language is violent and passionate and his actions are manic. Yet he still displays the sensitivity of before in granting Paris's request to be laid in the crypt:

> . . . O, give me thy hand,
> One writ with me in sour misfortune's book.
> I'll bury thee in a triumphant grave.

Conclusion

The central paragraphs of your answer should convey your opinions and should balance an outline of the action with critical commentary. Whether it is paragraph 2 or 3, the approach you use in writing should be similar, with each paragraph having a beginning, middle and end. However, each should deal with different stages of the scene and attempt to trace its development.

SAMPLE QUESTION AND ANSWER

QUESTION

Take any scene from a play studied by you and outline why you think that scene was important to the play, commenting on characterisation and dramatic impact. Your answer should contain suitable illustration to support your opinion.

ANSWER

The fight scene (Act III Scene I) in Shakespeare's *Romeo and Juliet* is a turning point in the play. In this scene, Mercutio, a friend of young Romeo of Montague, is killed by Tybalt of Capulet (Juliet's cousin). His death is avenged by a grief-stricken Romeo who is then banished. The deaths of Mercutio and Tybalt result in what was a lively and colourful play about young love becoming a tragedy, about revenge and Fate.

The scene begins comically. The irreverent Mercutio rejects the advice of his friend Benvolio to retire in case they meet Capulets, who are sworn enemies of the Montagues:

> And if we meet we shall not 'scape a brawl,
> For now these hot days is the mad blood stirring.

The arrival of Tybalt, the 'King of Cats', immediately introduces tension and suspense. When he requests: 'A word with one of you' Mercutio quips:

> And but one word with one of us? Couple it with
> something, make it a word and a blow.

The audience are aware that Tybalt will not tolerate the jibes and taunts of Mercutio. They are also aware that these two characters are anarchic and that disorder will be punished by Prince Escalus.

The arrival of Romeo, who has secretly married Tybalt's cousin Juliet, fills the audience with apprehension. Tybalt has previously sent Romeo a letter challenging him to a duel and now insults Romeo:

> Romeo, the love I bear thee can afford
> No better term than this: thou art a villain.

Here the dangers of the feud are fully dramatised. Tybalt's hatred is irrational and demands confrontation. It is this tension that makes the scene so riveting and which marks it as a climax in the play.

The death of Mercutio — which results from his anger at Tybalt mocking Romeo — is a shocking moment, filled with drama and pathos. Even facing death, Mercutio jokes about being a 'grave man' and that his wound is —

> . . . not so deep as a well, nor so wide as a
> church door; but 'tis enough, 'twill serve.

However, his curse on the two households is horrifying:

> A plague o' both your houses,
> They have made worms' meat of me.

This is the point where the play takes on a darker mood. Mercutio, the spirit of life and fun, is gone. The result is that Romeo momentarily curses Juliet for making him 'effeminate' and kills Tybalt in a rage of grief, which results in his banishment.

This scene is central to the play. It is the moment when the happiness of the lovers is doomed by the hatred of the feud.

General Observations

❧

ROMEO AND JULIET: THE RELATIONSHIP

When we first encounter Romeo he is a melancholic youth. It is significant that he is not involved in the opening fight, but has been wandering alone. This, along with his humour, separates him from the others in the play. His speech soon reveals that the unrequited love from which he suffers is not true love. When talking to Benvolio about his obsession he digresses to enquire where they will eat; he also expresses an interest in knowing about the fight that has occurred. Therefore, his preoccupation is not as all-consuming as it first appears. Most important, however, are both the form and content of what he says. He speaks in rhyme, often using heroic couplets, and what he says is filled with abstraction and oxymoron. Indeed, he rarely speaks of Rosaline — the cause of his melancholy — in terms of herself. Instead he speaks of the condition of love. It would appear then that he is role-playing: here is a youth who is in love with the idea of love.

This changes when he meets Juliet. The first thing she does is draw attention to his poverty of expression. She matches him with wit when he makes his initial 'pass' at her, demonstrating that she is aware of love's conventions. However, it is when he overhears her in the orchard that she shows the difference between real passion and role-playing. She rejects his exaggerated expressions of love and asks him to be true, to swear by himself alone. Her forthright comments initially confuse him. He is unable to express himself sincerely because he is trying to impress her. At this stage of their relationship she is very much in charge. It is she who first declares her love, who insists on a mode of expression that is sincere and who suggests that they get married the day after they meet.

The pace of the relationship frightens the Friar. He thinks that it will burn itself out because it is too intense. Indeed, it also frightens the lovers themselves at times. They become obsessed with each other as the ferocity of their passion overwhelms them. It certainly transforms both of them. Juliet goes from being an obedient and dutiful daughter to a disobedient, wilful child; while Romeo changes from a sophisticated, good-humoured youth to a rather primitive person whose actions become impulsive and violent, as he disregards public opinion.

We can measure Juliet's transformation in the way she becomes distanced from her parents, eventually rejecting even the companionship of the Nurse. Romeo's complete transformation may be gauged by comparing his opening speeches on love with his speeches in the graveyard and tomb at the end of the play. The latter are filled with violent images and are generally delivered in blank verse. Furthermore, Paris's presence in the play provides not only plot motivation but a contrast to Romeo. He is the kind of cultured, mannerly person Romeo once was. Looking at both of them in the graveyard is like confronting a gentleman and a savage.

It is important to note that the lovers always meet at night (expect for their marriage). They belong to a night world, a world of dream. They attempt to deny the existence of the feud by rejecting their true identities and by meeting when all others sleep. Theirs is a world within a world. The tragedy of the play is, therefore, realised in the imagination's inability to transform reality. Juliet may ask Romeo to deny it is day and that it is the lark they hear, but his declaration of complete love in agreeing is not enough to make this so. They are tied to the real world through family connections. The older generation will not be ignored and to this extent the play is a very real dramatisation of the generation gap, with hero and heroine as rebellious teenagers.

The play's ending is both a tragedy and a triumph. Juliet and Romeo have had to endure their suffering alone — he is in Mantua and she is bereft of reliable friends. While their deaths are horribly ironic in occurrence and tragic in consequence, they unite the community and finally allow the lovers to transcend reality.

MERCUTIO AND TYBALT

> What, drawn, and talk of peace? I hate the word,
> As I hate hell, all Montagues, and thee . . .

These words of Tybalt to Benvolio, among the first in the play, provide the audience with a clue to Tybalt's character. Here is an individual who delights in conflict. He scoffs at Benvolio's efforts to stop a quarrel, delighting in the confrontation that he has stumbled on. Indeed, it is his own entrance into the fray which invests it with a real sense of danger. Later, when Benvolio — the play's objective commentator — relates the incident to Montague, he emphasises Tybalt's 'fiery' and 'defiant' character. In many ways, Tybalt personifies the spirit of the feud: his actions are motivated by a senseless hatred, there is no purpose to them. It is merely violence for its own sake.

However, if Tybalt is the play's angel of death, waiting to wreak havoc wherever he goes (even at the feast of his uncle Capulet when Romeo's presence infuriates him), then Mercutio is the play's spirit of life. Mercutio is likewise a reckless person, but only in his disparagement of anything serious and in his dedication to fun. He is an intelligent, witty character with a zest for life.

His first appearance in the play sees him trading witticisms with Romeo, mocking the young lover's melancholic mood, a consequence of his unrequited love for Rosaline. Mercutio scorns such pining after women and advises Romeo,

> If love be rough with you, be rough with love;
> Prick love for pricking and you beat love down.

This advice contains an element of bawdiness. Mercutio's delight in puns, along with his carefree attitude, makes him an attractive character. Indeed, the essence of his wild and irreverent nature is exemplified in the Queen Mab speech. In this, a free rein is given to the imagination and Mercutio enters a trance-like state in the delivery of his mockery of love's dreams. It is a harmless, good-natured reverie, but Romeo is incisive in bringing it to a halt:

> Peace, peace, Mercutio, peace.
> Thou talk'st of nothing.

It is when Mercutio's thirst for the anarchic encounters Tybalt's unceasing quest for violent confrontation that the tragedy of the play occurs. The aims of both Tybalt and Mercutio are vivid in their physicality. Both are intensely passionate in the pursuit of their goal and stand in stark contrast to the hero and heroine. Mercutio's life is directed by whims of pleasure and a disregard for decorum, and so he scoffs at the thought of true love —

> . . . this drivelling love is like a great natural
> that runs lolling up and down to hide his bauble in
> a hole

and is contemptuous of Benvolio's advice to leave the market place before the Capulets' arrival. The eventual clash between Tybalt and Mercutio is somehow inevitable. Their reckless disregard for restrained conduct is a real threat to the lovers' happiness. The plot requires the tension of their meeting. Their natures, although opposite, share a delight in chaos which can only be truly satisfied in direct competition.

Initially, their meeting has comic overtones. Mercutio's sardonic rebuttal of Tybalt's insults are wonderful, and his mockery of Tybalt's swordsmanship is amusing. However, it is the arrival of Romeo which ironically brings danger with it. This lover of peace incites Tybalt's rage and irritates Mercutio with his vile submission to the villain. Mercutio recommences the dual and eventually Tybalt, unwittingly aided by an interfering Romeo, robs the play of its life, Mercutio. Romeo's subsequent killing of Tybalt seals the fate of the lovers. From this moment onwards the action of the play is determined by Mercutio's dying curse,

> A plague on both your houses,
> They have made worms' meat of me.

It is a cry of frustration and rage, shocking from a man who, at first, made fun of his wounds as 'a scratch, a scratch'.

In the figures of Mercutio and Tybalt the play discovers its sense of the dramatic. Whenever one of them is on stage, the audience pays extra attention. Mercutio delights us with his humour, while Tybalt frightens us with his hatred. Moreover, both characters in their ignorance of the love affair and their inability to comprehend true love invest the play with an almost unbearable pathos.

THE NURSE

The Nurse is a comic individual. She provides great fun in the play. She is garrulous, a female equivalent of Mercutio, and her vulgar jokes and innuendo annoy Lady Capulet when we first meet her in Act I Scene III. Later, in Act II Scene IV, she amuses us with her angry reaction to Mercutio's teasing, with the aloof manner she adopts when talking to Peter (her man) and in the way Romeo easily wins her over by rewarding her for acting as a messenger.

However, she also plays a vital role in the plot. She contributes to the tragedy because she allows the lovers to pursue a clandestine relationship that she knows would be forbidden by Juliet's parents. Yet, this is not what robs her of the audience's sympathy. It is her fickle and ultimately selfish and uneducated attitude that results in her being alienated from the audience.

The Nurse's idea of love is base. She thinks of love in purely sexual terms:

> Women grow by men . . .

Go, girl, seek happy nights to happy days. . . .

I am the drudge and toil in your delight
But you shall bear the burden soon at night.

When Juliet is being pressurised by her father to marry Paris (Act III Scene V), the Nurse does make some effort to intervene on her behalf; but when Capulet directs his anger at the Nurse and tells her to be quiet and to leave their company, she complies rather than tell the truth and risk incurring his wrath. The result is that the Nurse, Juliet's closest confidante, deserts her when she needs her most. She advises Juliet to forget Romeo and marry Paris for the sake of expedience. Her advice, of course, is immoral, taking no heed of loyalty or the sacredness of marriage. It displays a complete heartlessness in the matter of love. Juliet's reaction is to curse the Nurse privately, 'Ancient damnation! O most wicked fiend', and then to decide never to trust the Nurse again, 'Thou and my bosom henceforth shall be twain.'

Indeed, one can say of the Nurse that she is amoral. She seems to have no conscience and does not appear to make any distinction between right and wrong. It is her willingness to desert Juliet in order to protect herself that finally moves her from the realm of a comic character to a dangerous one. Certainly, an attitude that earlier in the play could have been regarded as funny (advising bigamy) is, in the latter stages of the tragedy, seen as insensitive and treacherous.

THEMES

LOVE AND HATE

The central theme of Shakespeare's *Romeo and Juliet* is that of a love which overcomes hate. Set in the Italian city of Verona, the play follows the fortunes of two teenage lovers, Romeo of Montague and Juliet of Capulet, whose families are involved in a deadly feud. The tragic plot depicts what happens when the two young people fall in love and marry secretly.

The seriousness of the feud is emphasised in the play's opening scene when members of both families become engaged in a street brawl. The incident is sparked by two Capulet servants, Gregory and Sampson, who taunt Abraham and Balthasar of the Montague house. This escalates into a street battle which involves young and old, including Capulet and Montague themselves, disrupting the peace of the city. Prince Escalus, in an effort to solve the problem, warns that the lives of those who 'disturb our street again . . . shall pay the forfeit of the peace'. From the moment of the Prince's edict, the actions of the characters are overshadowed by this warning and the action of the plot is imbued with suspense.

The lovers, however, are not involved in the street chaos, suggesting that they are apart from the violence that surrounds them. This idea of the lovers being distanced from the feuding of their families is also emphasised at the Capulet feast (Act I Scene V). Romeo has arrived in disguise with his friends. Upon seeing Juliet, he is enchanted by her and they begin a wooing sonnet that leads to their first kiss. Theirs is an innocent love that is born of mutual attraction. However, Juliet's cousin, the petulant Tybalt, recognises Romeo's voice, is enraged by a Montague daring to come 'to scorn at our solemnity this night', and is furious when his uncle forbids him to start a fight. Shakespeare uses this moment of conflict to illustrate the innocence of the lovers and, in doing so, contrasts the themes of love and hate. The light-hearted conversation of the lovers, which begins their clandestine affair, is overshadowed by Tybalt's scowl. In fact, this sets a pattern for the play, as from this point, Romeo and Juliet try, unsuccessfully, to distance themselves from the feud.

One character concerned with ending the feud is Friar Lawrence. Although he is concerned about the haste of the lovers' affair —

> These violent delights have violent ends
> And in their triumph die, like fire and powder,
> . . . love moderately;

he sees it as an opportunity to end the feud,

> For this alliance may so happy prove
> To turn your households' rancour to pure love.

However, his plans go dreadfully wrong when Romeo, drawn into the web of violence with the death of his friend Mercutio, kills Tybalt and is banished on his wedding day. The happiness of the lovers becomes more remote as society's obstacles surround them.

Act III Scene II begins with Juliet, an eager bride, awaiting news of her husband, and ends with the tragic news of his banishment. At first, Juliet is distraught and damns Romeo for killing Tybalt; but she regains her composure when she hears the Nurse also curse him. Juliet realises that her first loyalty is to her husband. For Juliet Romeo's banishment is like death and so death, not Romeo, will lie with her that night. All seems lost as the Nurse goes to find Romeo to bring him to Juliet for a 'last farewell'.

When Juliet's parents, who are unaware of her marriage to Romeo, insist upon an arranged marriage to Paris, a wealthy young suitor, the heroine risks even death to be true to love. She acquires a potion from the Friar that will feign death. She drinks this for the sake of love, 'Romeo, I come! This do I drink to thee!' When Romeo hears of Juliet's apparent death, he too prepares to sacrifice himself for love saying, 'Juliet, I will lie with thee tonight'.

The play's ending is both a tragedy and a triumph. Romeo and Juliet have had to endure their suffering alone: he in Mantua, she in Verona without friends or confidantes. While their deaths are a tragic consequence of ironic misunderstanding and due to the hands of Fate and Time, they unite the families and end the feud, bringing peace to Verona. Love finally overcomes hatred and the lovers' deaths allow them to transcend an unhappy reality that insisted on the separation of Capulet and Montague.

TIME

Time — along with the feud — is the real villain of Romeo and Juliet. Throughout the play the lovers are trying to outrun time and it plays a crucial part in the closing stages. For example, it is bad timing that results in Romeo being at the graveyard before he discovers the truth, and it is an accident of time that sees the Friar arriving too late to advise him. Furthermore, Juliet has two soliloquies which express her frustration with time. In Act II Scene V she is impatient that the nurse takes so long in bringing back word from Romeo about when they will be married and she wishes 'love's thought should be heralds', so that they could overcome distance and time. In Act III Scene II she is impatient that night should arrive so that she can be with Romeo. In fact, in this speech she tries to will night into being, attempting to overcome time with the power of the imagination.

Trying to outwit or outrun time is a theme that runs throughout the play. At the end of the balcony scene, the lovers part until the following morning, but Juliet says that 'tis twenty year till then'. For the lovers time apart is a lifetime and when they're together it flies. The coming of morning always separates them.

The climax of their attempt to defy reality, to ignore daily life in Verona (ruled by the feud), to disregard their names and to create an alternative world of their own comes in Act III Scene V. In this scene morning comes to separate the lovers after their wedding night. Juliet denies it is day and asks that Romeo remain with her. Here, Juliet tries to deny reality, refusing to allow time to separate them. Romeo complies with her wishes and agrees that it must be night if she wishes it so, knowing that it could mean losing his life. This is a wonderfully moving scene. In it, Romeo makes his most sincere declaration of love, allowing Juliet to decide his fate. Then she responds by admitting that it is dangerous for him to remain and advising him to go, even though it saddens her. At this point in the play, momentarily, the lovers imaginatively overcome reality and defeat time. It is a triumph of imagination, although it is short-lived.

Past Examination Questions

JUNIOR CERTIFICATE HIGHER LEVEL

1992

Answer (a) **or** (b)

(a) Basing your answer on ANY play studied by you, give an account of some scene or part of the play which you think would be most exciting or moving on stage. Give reasons for your answer.

You must give the playwright's name, and the title of the play that you choose.

or

(b) Choose an important scene in a play you have studied and show:
    (i) What it tells you about the principal character, and
    (ii) How that scene is related to the rest of the play.
    You must give the playwright's name and the title of the play that you choose.

1993

Answer (a) **or** (b) **or** (c) **or** (d)

(a) Basing your answer on ANY play studied by you, say whether you found the ending of the play credible or satisfying in the light of the action of the play as a whole.

You must give the playwright's name and the title of the play that you choose.

or

(b) Choose from ANY play studied by you the character that you felt had the strongest influence on the course of events in the play.

Explain by reference to the play why you chose this character.
You must give the playwright's name and the title of the play chosen.

or

(c) From the drama you have studied during your course, choose a scene which you consider highlights an important trait in one of the principal characters and show how this trait is displayed in that scene.
You must give the playwright's name and the title of the play that you choose.

or

(d) From the drama you have studied, choose a scene which portrays a strong disagreement between characters. Trace the cause of that disagreement and show how well the dramatist makes the disagreement come alive on stage. You are free, if you wish, to draw attention not only to what the characters say but also to the actions and the general presentation of the scene on stage.
You must give the playwright's name and the title of the play that you choose.

1994

Answer (a) **or** (b)

(a) Drama is excellent at creating an atmosphere or mood. Basing your answer on a play studied by you, describe a particular atmosphere or mood evoked in the play or in some part of it and discuss how that mood was created.
You must give the playwright's name and the title of the play that you choose.

or

(b) Drama is about relationships. Basing your answer on a play studied by you, discuss a key relationship that was examined in that play and describe how that relationship worked out in the end.
You should give the playwright's name and the name of the play that you choose.

1995

Basing your answer on a play studied in depth by you, answer (a) *or* (b) below.
NB: You must give the playwright's name and the title of the play that you choose.

(a) A play is nothing if it is not dramatic. Choose a play studied by you and describe the elements in it that made it interesting and compelling to watch.

or

(b) 1. Briefly describe two contrasting characters in a play you have studied.

    2. Pick one scene from the play in which this contrast is very clear and suggest how the contrast might be brought out in the production of the scene.

1996

Basing your answer on a play or film which you have studied discuss any ONE of the following:

1. The downfall of a great character and how it came about.
2. What I found to be humorous or funny in the film or play studied.
3. Aspects of the production that I liked, e.g. some of the following — acting, setting, scenery, lighting, costume, music, dance.

NB: You must give the name of the play or film that you choose.

1997

Select a play you have studied and use any two of the following starters, (a), (b), (c), (d), to write about your play.

(a) The things which make this play interesting to watch are . . .

(b) The audience would enjoy the scene in which . . . because . . .

(c) The play made me think more deeply about . . . because . . .

(d) I would like to play the part of . . . because . . .

NB: You must give the name of the play that you choose.

1998

Answer one of the following questions.

NB: You must give the name of the play or film that you choose.

1. 'Gripping drama often depicts a struggle/conflict between right and wrong, between good and evil'.

   Basing your answers on a play or film you have studied discuss this statement. You should support your answer by reference to at least two of the following:
   — the characters involved
   — how the struggle/conflict was dramatically portrayed on stage or screen
   — how the struggle/conflict was resolved.

   or

2. Cast a contemporary actor/actress in any role in a play you have studied. Justify why you cast this particular person in this role. You must name the play, playwright and the role to which you refer.

   or

3. Compare a stage or film version of a play you have studied with your impression of the play from the text. In your answer you should respond to the following:
   — what difference did you notice?
   — which version did you enjoy the more and why?

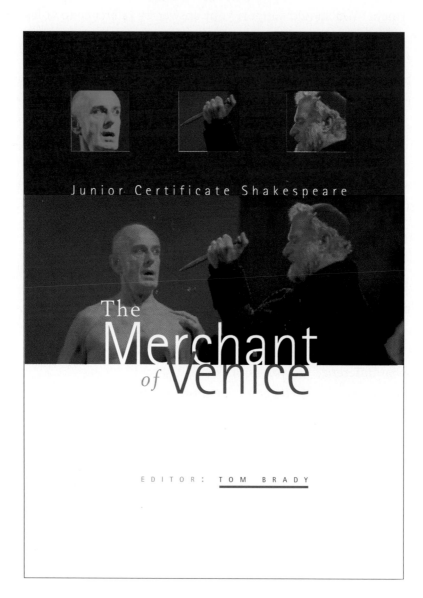